LIVES RELIVED

by

JOHN IVIMY

Pen Press Publishers Ltd
London

LIVES RELIVED

JOHN IVIMY

Second edition
First published 1996

A catalogue record of this book is available from the
British Library

ISBN 1 900796 32 5

Printed and bound in the U.K.
Published by Pen Press Ltd of London
39-41, North Road, London N7 9DP

CONTENTS

List of Illustrations

Our birth is but a sleep and a forgetting:
The Soul that rises with us, our life's Star,
Hath had elsewhere its setting.

William Wordsworth

I have been here before,
But when or how I cannot tell:
I know the grass beyond the door,
The sweet keen smell,
The sighing sound, the lights around the shore.

You have been mine before, -
How long ago I may not know:
But just when at that swallow's soar
Your neck turned so,
Some veil did fall, - I knew it all of yore.

Has this been thus before?
And shall not thus time's eddying flight
Still with our lives our love restore
In death's despite,
And day and night yield one delight once more?

Dante Gabriel Rossetti

I will come again.

Jesus

INTRODUCTION

The story was told in ancient Greece that when the mathematician Pythagoras (c.580 - c.500 B.C.) expounded to his disciples his theory of reincarnation he proved its validity by a personal experience of his own. He remembered, he said, that in his last life he had been a citizen of Troy named Euphorbus, who had died fighting for his country against the Greeks. He had been slain by Helen's husband Menelaus, who had taken his shield as a trophy and hung it among others in the temple of Hera in Argos. There Pythagoras, 600 years later, identified it as his own without having been told by the priests which one it was.

This is not a convincing story, and it is hard to believe that the philosopher's highly intelligent followers would have accepted it as proof of reincarnation. There was no shred of supporting evidence to connect Pythagoras with Euphorbus, about whose life and character nothing whatever was known.

In recent years many attempts have been made to substantiate the theory by similar subjective evidence, that is to say by means of records of personal experiences - some taken from subjects under hypnosis - in which people are claimed to have had 'far memories' from former lives of events of which they could not have acquired knowledge in this life. I find such claims unconvincing. But inadequate evidence does not invalidate a theory. If the theory is as important as this one surely is, promising as it does rewards and punishments hereafter to compensate for the injustices of our present lives, it only increases the need to search for truly convincing evidence.

In this book I have assembled, perhaps for the first time ever, a mass of hard historical facts which, taken all together, seem to me to make an irresistible case for concluding that the souls or psyches of certain well-known characters of classical antiquity returned to Earth to be born again centuries later. This purely objective evidence is provided by comparing their personalities, aims, achievements, and fortunes with those of the men and women of modern times whom I term their 'counterparts'. The book contains over a score of these comparisons, some in considerable detail but others only in brief outline. Together the points of coincidence they reveal are so numerous and often so improbable that I cannot see how any reasonable person could argue that they could *all* be due to chance.

If they are not all due to chance, there must be some causal connection between the souls of those great men of old and their modern counterparts. What connection could there be between two souls born up to twenty centuries apart in different countries and from different ethnic origins, unless they be one and the same soul in two different incarnations? That this is so is strikingly confirmed in a number of cases where portrait busts of the ancients have survived and show extraordinarily close resemblances to portraits of their counterparts.

The mere accumulation of factual evidence of a particular phenomenon does not, of course, explain it. For a rational explanation one needs a rational theory. No details have come down to us of the theory by which Pythagoras was able to explain reincarnation to his disciples because it was kept a close secret by that élite fellowship, the *mathematici*. The secret was lost when the Pythagorean brotherhoods which controlled the governments of a number of south Italian cities were massacred by democratic uprisings early in the fifth century B.C. But it was discovered again by Plato (c.428 - 347 B.C.), who worked it out for himself. He, too, kept it secret, even from his most brilliant pupil, Aristotle (384 - 322 B.C.). But the fact that the theory was never divulged does not mean that it is now impossible to reconstruct it.

By applying the famous 'theorem of Pythagoras' (which determines the relations between space in different dimensions) it is in fact possible to formulate a theory in multi-dimensional geometry which would offer rational explanations of how the psyche is related to the body, and how it is able to disengage itself from the body at death to orbit through higher dimensions and return to enter a new body at birth.

A detailed exposition of such a theory would be out of place in this book. Here it must suffice to summarise the main conclusions that can be deduced from it which are relevant to our theme. These constitute, in effect, a set of rules or guidelines that will help us in our search for useful examples of Lives Relived.

The comparison of two characters for the purpose of deciding whether or not they can be identified as one and the same is by no means a simple matter. It is not like comparing two geometrical shapes to see if the lines and angles of the one exactly coincide with the corresponding features of the other. Human psyches change in life and evolve in death as a result of efforts made or not made and of experiences suffered or enjoyed. Allowances must also be made for changes in the environments into which they are born in successive lives.

One cannot, therefore, lay down any hard and fast rules. There is, however, one overriding principle which applies in all cases: the principle of retributive justice. This follows from the basic Pythagorean doctrine that 'all things are number'. It means that our lives, like everything else in the universe, are governed by mathematical equations. Whatever we add to, or subtract from, the 'active' side of our life's equation has to be balanced, sooner or later, by a corresponding entry on the passive' side. Some of the many subtle ways in which this principle works out in practice from one life to another can be recognised in the biographical studies presented in this book.

Chapter One
THE GUIDELINES

Rules or generalisations to help us to identify recurrent souls can be deduced either from theory or from the accumulation of empirical evidence of individual cases. The following, derived from both sources, seem to me the most useful.

1.   The complete psyche or, as I prefer to call it, the 'psychosome' is a four-dimensional complex consisting of two intermeshing parts which animate the mind and the body respectively. (The three-dimensional body itself, which is left behind at death, may be said to constitute a third part in the living system.) After death the psychosome orbits in higher dimensions round the 'centre of gravity' of its particular culture, like a planet round the sun. If it leaves the world at a distance d from that centre it will re-enter the world after a half-orbit at a distance kd from that centre on the opposite side, where k is a coefficient of expansion which, in a period of expanding civilization is greater than 1. At the end of a half-orbit the two halves of the psychosome are transposed; after a full orbit they resume their former relative positions.

2.   The normal period of a half-orbit, as reckoned from birth to birth, of heavyweight souls in western civilization is between 500 and 600 years, making a full orbit of 1000 to 1200 years. This period, however began to increase to twice that length at the commencement of the Christian era.

3. The souls of men of action such as statesmen and soldiers (Type A souls) have longer and wider orbits than men of thought like poets and philosophers (Type C souls).

4. Men who amass wealth are born again correspondingly poor, whilst those who die poor but content will be born rich. The first in social status becomes last and the last first.

5. Good and evil deeds unrecompensed in one's current life are recompensed with added interest by apt rewards and punishments in a later life.

6. Errors which a man regrets having made in one life he instinctively avoids in later incarnations, whilst enterprises, just or unjust, which he found rewarding, his instinct will prompt him to repeat.

7. Desires which a man endeavours but fails to fulfil will be fulfilled for him with interest provided that he obeys the rules of his society; but if he tries prematurely to snatch a prize which, however unjustly, is denied him, it will be denied him again.

8. A man who shirks a hazardous or unpleasant duty will be confronted with a similar but greater ordeal in a later life, but he who strives and overcomes his fear will be born again naturally unafraid.

9. Physical skills and mental qualities that are acquired by effort in one life become innate natural talents and traits in the next; talents unused are lost.

10. Bodily characters can be affected by the experiences and mental proclivities of former lives. Physical defects about which a person is sensitive tend to be corrected in a later life, but over-sensitivity causes over-correction. Conceited men tend to be short; beauty that generates vanity is taken away. Muscular strength developed in one life and not used in the next turns to fat.

11.   Admiration of another's character may result in amalgamation with that other's soul during death and the reincarnation of the two souls as one. Conjugal fidelity and happiness in one life may lead to 'love at first sight' in the next.
12.   A very massive soul may split into two during death through sheer excess of spiritual size. Disintegration may also be caused by internal mental discord or failure to harmonise conflicts within the soul.

Knowledge of these rules may enable us to recognise a number of famous characters as they make successive appearances through the pages of history. As yet, however, detailed records rarely exist far enough back to enable their identity to be established beyond any reasonable doubt. The difficulty of recognition is aggravated by the fact that a man who appears the first time during a peak period of civilization makes his next half-orbital appearance during Dark Ages when reliable records are more than usually scarce.

With these reservations, the sets of characters described in following pages are offered as probable examples of reincarnate lives. In most cases the second life quoted is the first full-orbital reincarnation, the intermediate half-orbital life being omitted for lack of sufficient knowledge.

A list of the full-orbital lives is given in Appendix II below, numbered in the order in which they appear in the text, together with the orbital periods (i.e. the number of years between the two births) and the mean birth date. These are plotted on a graph in Appendix III. This shows the periods currently averaging about 1990 years for Type A characters and 1930 for Type C.

In deciding what geographical region to search for the re-birth of a particular character two points must be remembered.

The first is that Rule 1 above applies to half-orbits only. A person who died in the east at the end of life 1 will be re-born in the west after a half-orbit into life 2. He will be born again in the east into life 3 only if he ended life 2 in the west near where he was born then. If, therefore, due to lack of evidence we cannot identify him in life 2 it will be no more than a fair probability that his birth in life 3 will have occurred somewhere near where he died in life 1.

The second point is that throughout what I call the 'larval' or growing stage of world history from, say, 4320 B.C. to A.D. 1965 (when it entered the 'pupal' stage), the centre of gravity was moving west and north from the eastern Mediterranean to the English Channel. (See map) The centre carries with it souls that are in orbit round it. Therefore the latest incarnations of men who died close to the centre, say in Athens in 500 B.C. or in Rome in 50 B.C., should be looked for in France or England, assuming they remained close to the centre in intermediate lives.

Interleaved with the text I have included a number of illustrations which show clear facial resemblances between the ancient and the modern characters portrayed. These resemblances would appear to challenge the scientific view that our facial and other principal bodily characteristics are determined at conception by the genetic factors inherited from our parents, so that any likeness to people who lived centuries ago must be purely accidental.

My answer to this is that the theory of psychogenic evolution holds that physical characteristics are determined by the 'psychosome' which moulds the body in the shape it desires, within the limitations set by the biological conditions of the reproductive process. From conception to birth, the life of the foetus that causes it to develop in the womb is the vitality that was implanted in it by the parents when the ovum was

CYCLOIDAL CURVE marking the movement of the "Centre of
Gravity" of Western Civilization 4320 B.C. - 1965 A.D. (The numbered
divisions mark the beginnings of millennia + or - A.D.). The whole
cycle is 2π x 1000 = 6283 years.

fertilised, and the physical characteristics of the baby at birth are those which it inherited from its parents' genes. During that stage therefore the foetus has no 'personality' of its own. It is as much a part of its mother's body as her liver or her appendix. At birth, however, a psychosome returning from death enters the child's body and takes on the task of shaping its further development. If the psychosome is a strong and vigorous one, its somatic half, the 'anima', may cause the body to develop features quite unlike those of the biological parents - especially in the size and shape of the face and head, which house the psyche's most important physical machinery, the brain and the sense organs.

The prodigious genius of Shakespeare, for example, could only have been housed in a skull of which the shape and volume had been developed for that purpose from his infancy. It cannot be a mere chance coincidence that the shape of Shakespeare's head, as revealed in his portraits, was virtually the same as that of the like-minded Athenian dramatist, Aeschylus.

One last point. Comparisons of the names of many of these Greek and Roman characters with those of their modern counterparts show that in more cases than can reasonably be attributed to random chance, they bear a recognisable phonetic resemblance to one another. A note on this curious pheno-menon will be found in Appendix I.

Chapter Two

THE OLYMPIAN

Pericles (c.490 - 429 B.C.) = Marlborough (A.D.1650 - 1722)

It is one of the paradoxes of history that the period of antiquity that is commonly represented as the Golden Age of democracy, when the Parthenon was built and the free city of Athens reached the highest pinnacle of her splendour, was not really a period of democracy at all. It was the Age of Pericles when, as the Athenian historian Thucydides put it, "Athens, though still in name a democracy, was in fact ruled by her greatest citizen".

Born into a rich aristocratic family, Pericles was educated by the ablest and most advanced teachers of the day. The philosopher and scientist Anaxagoras taught him at an early age to direct his naturally keen intelligence along the lines of rationalist and scientific thought. His strong commonsense and well-balanced judgment were thus developed by careful training, and he learned in every situation to examine objectively and in detail all the facts before reaching a conclusion. All his life he remained free from any trace of political or religious prejudice.

Pericles was equally unmoved by any sentiment of personal pride or vanity. Simple, direct, and practical, he was able continuously to adjust his policies to suit the changing needs of the times. Nor was he constrained even by personal loyalties. Where lesser men would be prevented by vanity, prejudice, or party loyalty, from changing sides, Pericles could, with calm detachment, reverse the policy he had previously advocated and ally himself with those to whom he had formerly been opposed. He was a master of the art of having a foot in every camp. Having been instrumental in securing the banishment of the conservative leader Cimon, he did not hesitate to propose that statesman's recall a few years later when he saw that that course was then in the best interests of the Athenian people; and having risen to power by the votes of the popular party in the Assembly he never scrupled to pursue unpopular policies which he judged to be necessary. The one dominating motive throughout his life was the desire to make Athens great and to keep her people free.

Pericles had handsome features and a high forehead - so high in fact that it was caricatured by comic poets, and he was always depicted wearing a helmet - but he betrayed no trace of being conscious of his good looks. His manner was unaffected and his dress simple. He lived frugally and entertained not at all. His calm serenity and dignified bearing, together with the gravity of his words on the rare and always important occasions when he spoke in the Assembly, earned him the nickname of "the Olympian". Only once in his whole life was he known to give way to emotion. That was when his last surviving son was stricken to death by the plague, when he broke down and wept.

Both in his public and his private life one of Pericles' most outstanding qualities was his patience. It was as every statesman's should be, inexhaustible. This is well illustrated in a story told by Plutarch. On one occasion Pericles had been plagued all day in the conduct of public business by a tiresome wretch who continually heckled him, hurling vile reproaches and abuse. Pericles bore it all with unruffled composure. In the evening the man followed him home, shouting scurrilous insults at him all the way. Pericles appeared not to notice him. He said never a word, but when he arrived at his home, it being then dark, he sent one of his servants out with a torch to light the man home.

Pericles was married and his wife bore him two sons, but he divorced her after a short time and the greater part of his life he shared with Aspasia, a professional courtesan from Miletus of outstanding character and charm who was also a talented speaker in her own right, although women at that time could not speak in public.

In financial matters he was a man of scrupulous honesty and integrity - rare qualities at that time - but he was careful to the point of meanness in his expenditure. His estates were extensive, and although he never received a drachma for his services to the state, and though he was capable of generosity when occasion for it arose, his parsimony was such that by the end of his life he had saved a considerable fortune, and when he fell from power he was able to pay a very heavy fine. He quarrelled irrevocably with his eldest son because of the latter's extravagance.

During the greater part of his tenure of power in Athens Pericles pursued a policy of vigorous expansion, especially overseas, but his aggressiveness was tempered by prudence and he never undertook an expedition except after the most careful preparation. He personally commanded expeditions both on sea and on land and won a number of minor victories, but he showed no outstanding genius as a tactician and not all his ventures were successful.

When the war with Sparta was imminent Pericles did nothing to prevent it. It was as if he was suddenly unnerved by the realisation of the pass to which he had brought his country. His imperialism had aroused the hostility of the most powerful land power in Greece and now, mesmerised by the dragon he had awakened, he was unable to lift a finger to avert the impending disaster. For all his foresight he had manoeuvred the Athenians into a position from which they could neither successfully attack nor honourably withdraw. Switching over to a defensive policy he advised his people that if they avoided committing their forces in a land battle with the Spartans and confined their military effort to acts of retaliation from the sea victory would soon be theirs. The Spartans, he told them, had no money with which to support a war of attrition, and the patchwork Peloponnesian league would soon fall apart. The strength of Athens lay in her rich treasury and her overseas possessions. "Reflect," he said. "If we were islanders, who would be more invulnerable? Let us imagine that we are, and acting in that spirit let us give up lands and houses but keep a watch over the city and the sea."*

With these and other hollow arguments Pericles persuaded the people of Attica to leave their farms and villages and to crowd into Athens, bivouacking in the open spaces of the city and in the space between the long walls which joined it with the Piraeus. The Peloponnesians were thus able to invade Attica unopposed, burning the crops and the farmsteads and cutting down the precious olive orchards which take twenty years to mature, while the owners looked on helplessly from behind the city walls.

In the event, Pericles' policy proved utterly disastrous. The Spartans were perfectly capable of sustaining the burden of a long war, and they did far more damage to the Athenians by land than the latter could do to them by sea. Worst of all, in the second year of the war the plague broke out in Athens and spread like wildfire through the overcrowded city. The sufferings of the people were appalling. Upwards of 10,000 people died in dreadful agony. There was not a family which was not in mourning. The victims included Pericles' two sons, his sister, most of his other relations and friends, and lastly the great statesman himself.

* Thucydides I. 143; trans. Jowett

Plutarch records that as he lay on his deathbed, seemingly unconscious, his surviving friends were sitting round discussing his great deeds. In fact he was listening to every word, and at last he spoke: "I am surprised that while you dwell upon and extol these acts of mine, though fortune had her share in them and many other generals have performed the like, you take no notice of the greatest and most honourable part of my character, that no Athenian through my means ever put on mourning." *

Told in this way, this story does not ring true. In the first place, Pericles never boasted; and secondly, it was just not true that he had never been responsible for the death of an Athenian. On the contrary, he had led his people over and over again in enterprises in which many of them had been killed, and now it was because of his persuasion that thousands of Athenians had died, and were dying, of the plague. The whole city was in mourning because of him. Plutarch surely missed the point of the story. With a little imagination perhaps we can reconstruct the train of thought that was passing through the Olympian's mind as he lay on his deathbed.

Pericles had always been acutely self-critical. He aimed at perfection and was content with nothing less. When anything went wrong his first reaction was not to attribute the fault to others or to blame it on bad luck or divine opposition, but rather to enquire critically whether the failure could have been avoided if he himself had acted differently. This was the clue to his greatness, because in this way he learned in one lesson what lesser men learn in three or four.

So now, as he lay dying, he was overwhelmed with remorse at the tragedy for which he took all the blame upon himself. His whole life's work, the work of making Athens great, lay

* Plutarch: *Life of Pericles*; trans. Langhorne

11

in ruins about him. With the prophetic vision of a man close to death he could see the war stretching on and on into the future, with Athens becoming weaker as her enemies grew stronger, and having no means of winning a swift and decisive victory. Already the unity which he had established in the management of national policy was riven by squabblings and petty jealousies, and there was no wise leader to follow him. After the second invasion of Attica in the previous year, during which he had led a futile naval expedition to ravage the coast of the Peloponnese, the people had turned on him. They had removed him from office, fined him heavily, and then sent envoys to Sparta to sue for peace. But the terms offered them were too harsh and they had to continue the war, so they had elected Pericles general once more.

But it was then too late for him to change his policy. How bitterly now he reproached himself for ever having adopted it. "How safe we would be if we were islanders" he had said, "let us therefore pretend that we are." Of all the sayings of great statesmen recorded in history, surely this takes the prize for sheer stupidity. He recalled it now with shame. It was so unlike him, too, not to face the facts as they were. Why had he been so blind?

Looking now calmly into the inmost recesses of his own mind he saw the reason for his folly. It was fear. He had been afraid of the fame and prowess of the Spartan army, and he had mistrusted his own competence as a general and the capacity of the Athenian people to fight on land. With the wisdom of hindsight he saw what he should have done. While there was yet time he should have trained and equipped an Athenian army to defend Attica against invasion. Then when King Archidamus brought his Spartans to the attack he could have led his people out to crush them in a pitched battle. With their farmsteads and their families to defend, the Athenians would have fought like heroes. He had forgotten how they had conquered the Persian host at Marathon. One or two such battles and he would have been able to negotiate an honourable peace. Even if Athens had been defeated, the city would have been in no worse plight than it was in now. At least there would have been glory in fighting where there was nothing but shame in sheltering behind walls and letting the enemy wreak destruction unopposed.

Such must have been the thoughts that passed through Pericles' mind as he lay dying and which he was to take with him across the Styx. So it was in a mood of self-reproach and bitter irony that, when he heard his friends talking about his life, he said: "I notice you do not say that no Athenian ever put on mourning because of what I did."

In the distinctive character of John Churchill, first Duke of Marlborough, can be discerned all the essential features of the character of Pericles.

Born of a well-connected but impecunious family in the west of England in the first year of the Commonwealth, John Churchill spent his early years in poverty. His father, Winston Churchill, had been fined for fighting in the Royalist cause in the Civil War, and for the first ten years of John's life the family was forced to share the half-ruined house of Winston's mother-in-law on whose meagre bounty they subsisted. But when the monarchy was restored in 1660 the Churchill fortunes improved, and as soon as John left school he entered the life of the Royal Court as page to the Duke of York, who was afterwards King James II. Here "his personality unfolded with remorseless assurance, sometimes in harmony with but as often in opposition to its environment". *

* Winston S. Churchill: *Marlborough, his Life and Times.*

13

All the Periclean traits of character develop one by one: the calm dignity and serene composure, the patience, the simplicity and total absence of personal vanity or affectation, the compassion, tact, and gentle humanity, the natural thriftiness, this time strongly encouraged by the early experience of poverty but still tempered by generosity when occasion arose, the commonsense, rationalism, and open-minded attitude to religion, and the objective detachment with which all facts are studied in close detail before a decision is made. We see also the lofty detachment from personal or party ties that enabled Marlborough, who owed his first preferments and professed himself devoted to James II, to become the leading figure in the rebellion by which that King was deposed, and later to correspond with him in exile so as to be prepared, should it at any time prove to be in the best interests of the English people, to procure his return.

The noble countenance of Pericles, as portrayed in marble during his lifetime by the Cretan sculptor Cresilas, is easily recognisable in the handsome features of the Duke of Marlborough as recorded in contemporary paintings. The high forehead is still there, though this time not so abnormally high as to attract unwelcome attention. What Sir Winston Churchill wrote of his great ancestor's portrait could with equal aptitude have been written of the Athenian statesman: "the comprehending, appraising, slightly mocking expression of the lips and nostrils - indeed of the whole face - the symmetry of the features, and the sense of Olympian calm linger with us, and offer their own explanation of the influence he exerted upon all with whom he came into contact." *

* Winston S. Churchill.

PERICLES

MARLBOROUGH

The same author tells a story of Marlborough's imperturbable self-control that echoes the tale told by Plutarch about Pericles. It concerns the Duke's relations with his wife, Sarah.

One day in passionate disagreement with her husband she determined to cut off the long locks of hair which he so much admired.

> ". . . Instantly the deed was done. She cropped them short and laid them in an antechamber he must pass through to enter her apartments. To her cruel disappointment, he passed, entered, and repassed cool enough to provoke a saint; neither angry nor sorrowful: seemingly quite unconscious of his crime and his punishment. Concluding he must have overlooked the hair she ran to secure it. Lo! it had vanished. And she remained in great perplexity the rest of the day. The next as he continued silent, and her looking glass spoke the change a rueful one, she began for once to think she had done a foolish thing . . ."

It was only after his death that she discovered her locks in the secret cabinet where he kept his greatest personal treasures.

But while the personality is the same, how different were the deeds and fortunes of the two men! Pericles had wished with all his heart that his country had been an island, and he had acted as if it were. Marlborough's country really was an island, but throughout the period during which his voice was a deciding influence in English policy, that policy was conducted as if England were a continental power.

Marlborough had a natural understanding of naval matters that was rare in a general, but when war came with France - a war which he was principally instrumental in provoking - he insisted that his country must fight on land and send an army into Europe. There was in fact no pressing need for England to become involved on the continent in the War of the Spanish Succession. The country was not in danger and the small contingent of 12,000 men which was all that Marlborough was able to take with him, added little to the strength of the Austrian and Dutch armies on whom the brunt of the fighting must necessarily fall. England's long-term interests lay in developing her naval power, in expanding her trade and colonies overseas, and in securing bases from which to conduct the struggle with France that must come later in theatres far away from Europe.

Marlborough was, of course, afraid of the mighty armies of Louis XIV. Who would not be? To engage the Grand Monarque on territory of his own choice with a motley assembly of men of different languages and military traditions, commanders pursuing conflicting objectives and hampered by political control from different capitals, and all the disadvantages of exterior lines and bad communications, was an enterprise fraught with the utmost peril. Had it failed the historians would doubtless have dubbed it foolhardy. But despite the dangers, Marlborough took his courage in both hands and decided to attack the French on land and bring the issue to a head in a pitched battle. So he set out on his famous march to the Danube, and on the battlefield of Blenheim in 1704 he began the task of repairing the costly blunder that he had made twenty-one centuries before.

But the France of Louis XIV was a much more formidable adversary than the Sparta of Archidamus. In ten campaigns Marlborough engaged the French armies winning victory after victory, but at the end of it all he was still denied the prize. In 1711 he was recalled to England, accused of peculation, stripped of his offices, and disgraced.

For this reversal of fortune the person principally responsible was a woman, Abigail Masham, lady of the bedchamber to Queen Anne. Inspired by jealousy and hatred of her cousin and benefactress Sarah, Duchess of Marlborough, Mrs Masham had undermined the Duke's influence with the Queen. In the hostility of these two women do we not hear an echo of the clash that surely took place in the household of Pericles when he divorced his wife and took Aspasia as his mistress? We know nothing about the wife's character. But what we know of the influence which Aspasia exercised in Athens through her beauty and charm, her forceful personality and her political sagacity - even Socrates enjoyed listening to her discourses - is sufficient to enable a fair comparison to be made with that exercised in England by the Duchess of Marlborough.

The Duke's profound and life-long love for Sarah in an age of dissolute morals and marital infidelities is the more readily understandable if we believe it to have been deeply rooted in the hidden memories of a former life. Further, the fact that Sarah had befriended Abigail when the latter was in need, and that it was the Duchess's compassion and generosity that was responsible for Mrs. Masham's position at Court, all fits into the pattern. In Sarah's concern for Abigail we recognise the mistress seeking instinctively to make amends for the wrong she had done the wife; and in Abigail's calumniation of Marlborough we see the injured wife taking revenge on the unfaithful husband.

If Marlborough's downfall through the intrigues of Mrs Masham was an example of divine justice exacting retribution for the misdeed of a former life, it was apparently not the only one in the general's career. As we have seen, it was thanks to Pericles' timorous counsel that thousands of Athenians had died in the plague. For this it was not sufficient that the statesman himself, his two legitimate sons, his sister and most of his relatives should perish, but in his next life he had to suffer the bitterest blow of all - the loss of his eldest and only surviving son, John Churchill, Marquess of Blandford. A boy of brilliant promise, John was pursuing his studies at Cambridge when he fell a victim to the current epidemic of smallpox. His death nearly broke his father's heart.

Chapter Three
THE ICONOCLAST

Alcibiades (c.450 - 404 B.C.) = Peter the Great
(A.D. 1672 - 1725)

There could scarcely be a greater contrast than that between the character and deeds of Pericles and those of his young kinsman and ward Alcibiades, whose influence was one of the dominating factors in the latter part of the Peloponnesian War. Whereas the former excelled in patience, thrift, and self-control, the latter was impetuous, extravagant, and fiery-tempered; whilst the integrity and forbearance of the one were matched by the duplicity and vindictiveness of the other. A story of Plutarch's points the contrast. One day when young Alcibiades went to call on his guardian he was not permitted to enter because Pericles was working on the accounts he had to present to the Athenian people. "If I were in his position," said the youth to the servant at the door. "I would be working out how to avoid having to present any accounts at all." It was in that spirit that Alcibiades conducted his life and made his mark on history. It was a mark of some consequence. The city that the older man made great the young man brought to ruin.

Alcibiades was born in Athens the heir to a large fortune and the possessor of outstanding physical beauty, strength, energy, and natural talents. As a boy and throughout his life his ruling passion was the desire to dominate. Whether in games or in politics he had to win, and if he could not win by fair means he won by foul - a character that made him admirably suited for the position of war leader to which he aspired. He loved the limelight and enjoyed the feeling that he was feared. His nature was not free from cruelty and he had a certain ghoulish sense of humour. Once he bought an enormous and very expensive dog with a magnificent tail; then, according to Plutarch, he cut off its tail for no other purpose than to get himself talked about. (But I shall suggest presently an alternative version of this unlikely story.)

Alcibiades never did anything by halves. Whatever enterprise he undertook he threw himself into whole-heartedly and he made it his object to outdo everyone else. His ideas were conceived on a vast and grandiose scale. When he entered for the chariot race at Olympia he did not enter one or even two chariots but seven, a number never equalled before or after even by a king, let alone by a private citizen. Typically, he carried off the first, second, and fourth prizes.

Such flamboyant ostentation, combined with sudden displays of spontaneous generosity, endeared Alcibiades to large numbers of the common people; but his wild extravagance, unruly behaviour, and his adoption of un-Athenian ways and manners made him many enemies amongst the more conservative Athenians.

When the Peloponnesian war broke out, Alcibiades was about nineteen. Socrates, some twenty years older, was then acquiring fame as the teacher of a new morality, questioning traditional views on religion and ethics, shaking people out of their complacent orthodoxy and goading them into thinking for themselves rationally and objectively. The two men became close friends; serving together in the army, and for a while Socrates exercised a strong moderating influence on the younger man. He seems to have been the only man for whom Alcibiades ever had any true respect. The latter's exuberant thirst for pleasure, which from time to time he indulged with a band of followers in Bacchanalian revels, was sensibly restrained by the kindly reproofs and austere example of the philosopher.

After ten years of war an uneasy peace was patched up between Athens and Sparta. It was then that Alcibiades made his political début. Moved either by patriotism or personal ambition or both, and jealous of the Athenian general Nicias who was responsible for the peace, he allied himself with the war party and proposed an alliance with the Peloponnesian city of Argos. He saw clearly the weakness of the Periclean policy and insisted that Athens must develop strength as a land power if she was to maintain her empire.

The Spartans feared the proposed Athens-Argos alliance and sent envoys to dissuade the Athenians from concluding it. The envoys first addressed the Athenian Senate, whom they informed that they came as plenipotentiaries armed with full powers to negotiate. They made a favourable impression. Fearing they might also win over the Assembly, Alcibiades resorted to a trick. He took them on one side and, pretending to be friendly to their cause, he gave them to understand that he would support them and they could get what they wanted if they told the Assembly that they had not got full powers to negotiate. When, accordingly, they were introduced to the Assembly and were asked if they had full powers, they said No. Alcibiades promptly rose to his feet, informed the people that the envoys had just said the opposite to the Senate, accused them of double-dealing and so incensed the people against them that their mission fell through.

This was one of a number of examples of Alcibiades' duplicity. But although he was deceitful in his dealings with his enemies, there is no evidence that he was ever guilty of breaking an unequivocal promise, or that in his relations with those who for the time being were his friends he was anything but fair and honest. The Athenian people as a whole did not trust him because they thought not that he was dishonest but that he was too ambitious for power, while the conservatives hated him for his unorthodox morality and his iconoclastic ideas. It was they who stirred up the people's mistrust of his ambition. Nevertheless, his dynamic energy, his eloquence, and his exceptional talents made it impossible for them to ignore him, and when the great expedition to Sicily which he amongst others had advocated was voted, he was elected one of its three commanders-in-chief. Nicias, who had opposed it, was one of the other two.

The Sicilian expedition was the mightiest armada that had set out from the shores of Greece since Agamemnon sailed for Troy. Its object was to establish an Athenian land empire in the west (which might be extended in due course to North Africa), and thence to return to conquer the Peloponnese. No sooner, however, had the expedition arrived at its destination than Alcibiades was recalled to Athens to answer charges of desecration and impiety.

Shortly before the expedition sailed a number of statues of the god Hermes which stood at the doorways of temples and private houses in Athens had been mutilated. It was further alleged that Alcibiades and his band of followers had mimicked the Eleusinian Mysteries, sacred to the goddess Demeter, in one of their drunken revels. A mock procession had been held in which Alcibiades had been comically dressed up as the high priest.

Knowing that these charges were hanging over his head, Alcibiades demanded to be tried before the expedition set sail. But his enemies were too clever to allow him that advantage. They let him go. Then, with the army and all his supporters out of the way they recalled him to stand his trial, having first decreed severe punishments for anyone found guilty of these crimes against the established religion.

When Alcibiades received the order for his return there were three courses open for him to consider. He could obey the order and return to stand his trial; he could return at the head of his fleet and seize power in Athens by force; or he could escape and go into voluntary exile. Knowing the strength of his enemies in the city, Alcibiades had no doubt that the first course would lead to his condemnation and execution. The second course, though the most attractive to his ambitious nature, was impracticable because, unlike Julius Caesar at the Rubicon, he only commanded a third of the forces present with him, and Nicias and the other commander were opposed to him. He therefore adopted the third course, escaped from those who were sent to arrest him and took refuge with his country's enemies.

The Athenians condemned Alcibiades to death in his absence. For this he took a terrible revenge. Having gained influence with the government of Sparta he persuaded them to take a number of military measures designed to checkmate his country's ambitions in Sicily and to threaten her security at home. Thanks to these measures, the mighty Athenian armada was utterly destroyed in the second year after it set out. Over 30,000 men were killed or taken prisoner, and a Spartan garrison was established in Attica on a permanent basis within sight of the Acropolis. Not content with this, Alcibiades got himself appointed to the command of a Poloponnesian naval squadron sent out to stir the Athenian dependencies in Ionia to revolt. Again he was successful, and the Athenian empire in the eastern Aegean was brought to the brink of dissolution. Only one important base remained to them: the island of Samos.

The method by which Alcibiades obtained influence with the Spartans, and later with the Persians, is significant. It is described by Plutarch as follows:

"By conforming to their [the Spartans'] diet and other austerities, he charmed and captivated the people. When they saw him close shaved, bathing in cold water, feeding on their coarse bread, or eating their black broth, they could hardly believe that such a man had ever kept a cook in his house, seen a perfumer, or worn a robe of Milesian purple. It seems that amongst his other qualifications, he had the very extraordinary art of engaging the affections of those with whom he conversed, by imitating and adopting their customs and way of living. Nay, he turned himself into all manner of forms with more ease than the chameleon changes his colour. It is not, we are told, in that animal's power to assume a white, but Alcibiades could adapt himself either to good or bad, and did not find anything which he attempted impracticable. Thus at Sparta he was all for exercise, frugal in his diet, and severe in his manners. In Asia he was as much for mirth and pleasure, luxury and ease. In Thrace, again, riding and drinking were his favourite amusements: and in the palace of Tissaphernes, the Persian grandee, he outvied the Persians themselves in pomp and splendour. Not that he could with so much ease change his real manners, or approve in his heart the form which he assumed; but because he knew that his native manners would be unacceptable to those whom he happened to be with, he immediately conformed to the ways and fashions of whatever place he came to. When he was at Lacedaemon, if you regarded only his outside, you would say as the proverb does, 'This is not the son of Achilles, but Achilles himself; this man has surely been brought up under the eye of Lycurgus:' but then if you looked more nearly into his disposition and his actions, you would exclaim, with Electra in the poem, 'The same weak woman still!'*

* Plutarch: *Life of Alcibiades*, trans. Langhorne. The quotation is from the *Orestes* of Euripides.

The last remark refers to the fact that, dependent though he was on the hospitality of the Spartan government, he could not resist the temptation to seduce the wife of their King Agis. To the jealousy that had already been aroused by his popular successes was now added the personal animosity of the Spartan king, and while Alcibiades was with the squadron in Miletus orders came from Sparta that he should be put to death.

He now fled to the court of Tissaphernes, the Persian satrap of Sardis who, thanks largely to his instigation, had been drawn into an alliance with Sparta. Having satisfied his vengeance against Athens Alcibiades now proceeded to revenge himself on the Spartans and set about inducing Tissaphernes to change sides. Before long he was invited to take command of the Athenian fleet in the eastern Aegean which was based at Samos. Through a series of naval victories over the Spartans during the next four years he won back for Athens nearly all her lost possessions in Ionia and had secured for her the command of the entrance to the Black Sea.

In 407 B.C., Alcibiades made a triumphant entry into Athens where he was received with enthusiasm, solemnly freed from the curse that had been laid on him for profaning the Mysteries, and was decreed full powers for the conduct of the war. According to Plutarch, the people even put a golden crown on his head. Had he so decided he might now have set himself up as tyrant of Athens, but he made no attempt to do so. If, however, he thought that the Athenian people had learnt their lesson, he was mistaken. The same year, after his fleet had suffered a slight reverse for which he was not even personally responsible, he was relieved of his command.

Once more in exile, Alcibiades collected a band of followers together and went to Thrace where he lived as a freebooter, riding and drinking and conducting a private war against barbarian tribes. Three years later, from his castle near the coast he watched the final defeat of his people at the hands of the Spartan admiral Lysander, at the decisive battle of Aegospotami. He could and would have saved his country in this last extremity if the Athenian admirals had not insulted him when he tried to warn them of the weakness of their position.

Persecuted and friendless he took himself again to the dominions of the King of Persia. The Spartans were now absolute masters of Greece by sea and land, but such was the fear inspired in them, and such were the hopes raised in the minds of the defeated Athenians by even the remote possibility that Alcibiades might one day return to Athens, that Lysander was ordered to arrange with the Persians to have him killed. The assassins who were sent to do the deed dared not attack him from close at hand, so afraid were they of his great strength and tempestuous rage, so they set about killing him as if he were a wild beast. They set fire to the house where he was living with his mistress Timandra in a village in Phrygia, and when he came out they showered arrows on him from a distance. He was about forty-six years old when he died.

Alcibiades died in the east, far from his native Greece, so we must look for the return of that dynamic soul somewhere in eastern Europe or western Asia on the borders of western culture. The date of his birth should be about a generation later than that of the Duke of Marlborough. As to his estate, no man ever desired power more eagerly and was more unfairly frustrated in his ambition than Alcibiades, but he played the game according to the rules of his society. He made no attempt to seize power for himself by force. In accordance with the guide-lines of the reincarnation process therefore, we may expect to find him in his next life born to a position of great power.

All these requirements are met in the person of the Russian Czar Peter the Great. Born in Moscow in 1672, Peter was elected Czar of Muscovy at the age of ten. In 1721, after he had extended the frontiers of his kingdom to gain access to the Black Sea in the south and the Baltic in the north, he was proclaimed 'Emperor of All the Russias' the absolute ruler of the vastest empire in the world.

A handsome giant six feet six inches tall, so strong that he could straighten a horse-shoe with his bare hands, and endowed with prodigious energy, Peter the Great answers exactly to the descriptions we have of the physical characteristics of Alcibiades. In him, too, we see the Athenian's restless enquiring mind, his fiery temper, and his dominating will. These dynamic qualities are more typical of the west than of the east, and utterly unlike those that were to be found either in the lazy, ignorant, servile Muscovite people of the seventeenth century or in the weak, pious, conservative family of the Romanoff czars into which Peter was born.* Even more untypical of his Muscovite heritage was Peter's lifelong and absorbing passion for the sea and ships and all things nautical - an instinct that surely betrays its origin in a former life's experience as the successful admiral of a great sea power.

---

* Peter's father, the Romanoff Czar Alexius Mikhailovich, was a weak character whose other children (by his first wife) "had shown from infancy signs of ugliness and degeneracy." Peter, the son of his second wife, was born "a model of vigour, beauty, and liveliness - all it took for the palace scandalmongers to call into question Peter's paternity." According to contemporary rumours, Peter's mother, Czarina Natalya, had many lovers, one of whom was the Patriarch Nikon, whom Peter resembled in his physique, and another was a courtier of humble extraction, Tikhon Streshnev whom he resembled in intelligence and strength of will. (Henri Troyat : *Peter the Great*, translated from the French by Joan Pinkham, Hamish Hamilton 1988, p.7.)

Like Alcibiades, Peter threw himself wholeheartedly and with irresistible ardour into every enterprise he undertook, never sparing himself nor those around him. Whatever he did was done regardless of cost, on a tremendous scale. He drank hard and could indulge again and again in wild bacchanalian orgies apparently without detriment to his health or vigour; rather, they refreshed him for his next day's work. He displayed, too, both the Athenian's vindictiveness and his duplicity in dealings with his enemies; and his possession of absolute power enabled him to give a free rein to the streak of cruelty and the macabre sense of humour which, in Alcibiades, had been inhibited by his position as a private citizen.

At the age of ten Peter, an intelligent boy who was old for his years and gifted with a lively imagination, suffered a terrible shock to his nervous system. He and his half-brother Ivan had just succeeded to the throne as joint czars when there occurred a revolt of the *streltsi*, the soldiers who acted as police in Moscow and who mounted guard at the Kremlin. In a raging mob they stormed up the steps on top of which Peter was standing with his mother, tore his distinguished friend and chief minister Matveev from his side, and threw the unfortunate man down on to the pikes of the men below who hacked him to pieces before the boy's terrified eyes. The colonel of the regiment who tried to discipline them was similarly butchered. It seems that the Czar's nervous system never recovered from the trauma of that experience, which is considered to have been responsible "for the mad rages that in later years would suddenly seize him, making it unsafe to be near him, and for the ugly twitching that contorted his handsome face throughout his life". *

* Ian Gray: *Peter the Great*: Hodder & Stoughton, 1962.

The course of Peter's mental development through adolescence and early manhood followed the same pattern as that of Alcibiades. The latter's friendship with Socrates was parallelled by Peter's friendship with the jovial Swiss adventurer Franz Lefort. Both attachments were symptoms of the young man's eager thirst for knowledge and the pleasure that he derived from the exploration and discussion of new ideas. Socrates and Lefort were very different characters, but they had this in common: both were free-thinkers with a hatred of bigotry, dogmatism, and religious intolerance. The former died for the right of young men to think for themselves; the latter was a refugee from the suffocating inhumanity of calvinistic Geneva. But whereas Socrates developed his stimulating new ideas on abstract subjects such as justice, virtue, and love, Lefort was the medium through whom Peter obtained access to the new and exciting world of science and engineering that was blossoming out of the invention of analytical geometry and the infinitesimal calculus. Lefort was not a learned man, but he had a wide superficial knowledge of many subjects, and he lived in the foreign quarter of Moscow which Peter early recognised as the only oasis of spiritual enlightenment that was to be found in the whole of Muscovy. He was also an excellent drinking companion.

Beginning with Lefort, Peter attracted round himself a band of free-thinking hard-drinking high-spirited young men which he named "The Synod of Fools and Jesters." Its object was to ridicule the rites and ceremonies of the Russian Orthodox and Roman Catholic churches by celebrating instead the cult of Bacchus "with frequent and abundant libations." At the head of this company of drunkards he placed the biggest drunkard of all, his former tutor Nikita Zotov, who was awarded the title "Prince Pope" or "Prince Patriarch." To enable him to play his role, Zotov was given a salary of two thousand roubles, a palace, and twelve servants, all of whom were stutterers. During the "ceremonies" he wore a tin mitre and carried a tin sceptre, spewed forth incoherent speeches in which obscenities alternated with quotations from the Bible, and blessed the company that knelt before him with two long Dutch pipes, hitting them on the head with a pig's bladder. Then he would give them, as an icon to kiss, an indecent statue of Bacchus. He would dance before them, staggering and belching, tucking his sacerdotal robes up over his bandy legs. The Prince Pope was surrounded by a college of twelve cardinals and a great many mock bishops, mock archimandrites, and mock deacons, all inveterate guzzlers and gluttons. The Czar himself played the archdeacon. He attended all the meetings and drank more than anyone else. With his own hand he drew up the statutes of the order, established the hierarchy of its members, and specified the smallest details of the sacrilegious performances."*

The parallel between Peter's mockery of the rites of the Christian Church and Alcibiades' profanation of the Eleusinian Mysteries is obvious. It may be asked why, seeing that the offence he gave his compatriots in Athens when he ridiculed the mumbo-jumbo of their rites and ceremonies had helped to cause his downfall there, he had not learned his lesson. Why was he not instinctively impelled to avoid repeating the same crimes against religion in his next life? The answer I suggest is that Alcibiades never for a moment regretted his action. The search for truth was his creed - the creed he had learned from Socrates - and to him therefore the established religion of the Greeks, especially the worship of Demeter, the most primitive of all Greek deities, was like the antichrist, for it stood in the way of advancing knowledge. Peter, like Alcibiades, realised

* H. Troyat : loc, cit. p.71.

that ancient religious rituals and worn-out dogmas which are popularly regarded as sacred and are sanctioned by the state, are hindrances to intellectual progress, and that the best way of stripping from them their cloak of sanctity was to hold them up to ridicule.

In his battle with the pietists of Athens, Alcibiades was defeated, but the subconscious memory of that defeat only made Peter the more determined to break the spiritual power of the Church in Muscovy and to set the Russian people free from the religious obscurantism by which their spirit had for centuries been shackled. In this Peter was not wholly successful, but neither was he defeated. The conservative core of the Orthodox Church hierarchy abhorred him and would have compassed his downfall if they could, but he saw to it that they were leaderless, and he forced them against their will to accept a number of reforms, notably in the field of education, designed to blow fresh air through the musty sanctuaries which till then had been hermetically sealed against external influence.

In politics Peter showed the same aggressive and progressive spirit as in matters of religion. Despite his enjoyment of autocratic powers he had an instinctive feeling towards measures of popular self-government. He never contemplated giving the people any share in the control of national policy, but he did introduce a measure of democracy into the machinery of local government.

In his first military campaign in 1695, in which he tried to capture Azov from the Turks, Peter seems to have been haunted by a forgotten memory of his experience as a general of the Athenian democracy in 414 B.C. For no reason known to history, Peter divided his army into three parts each under an independent commander, and left the overall strategy to be decided by agreement between them, whilst he himself served in a subordinate command. Did he perhaps subconsciously remember how a similar arrangement had prevented him from defying the legitimate authorities in Athens when they had tried to recall him, and was he subconsciously fearful lest another man whom he might appoint as supreme commander might use his position to conduct a successful rebellion against himself? That he avoided taking the command himself on this and on later occasions, at least until after he had proved himself at the battle of Lesnaya in 1708, was no doubt due to the consciousness of his inexperience of land warfare, for Alcibiades had never commanded an army in an important battle.

Despite his territorial conquests Peter the Great was not by instinct a conqueror. His aim was to regenerate Russia and to build a nation that could compete commercially and culturally on equal terms with the rest of Europe. It was in pursuit of that aim that he fought Turkey and Sweden, extended the frontiers of his realm to the Black Sea and the Baltic, built the great city of St. Petersburg and created the Russian navies.

The critical point of his career, when he took the measure of the herculean task which he had set himself, was the great tour of Europe that he made in 1697-8 when he was twenty-five years old. He visited many countries and displayed in each the chameleon-like adaptability which had distinguished Alcibiades in his journeyings through Greece and Asia. In Amsterdam he worked for four months in a shipyard on the construction of a frigate. He dressed and lived like an ordinary workman, wielding hammer and saw and learning how to make masts, blocks, ropes, and sails. When the whaling fleet came in he did not mind the stench and filth but clambered below decks to see how the ships were constructed. In England he conversed and drank on equal terms with merchants and technicians, with ships' captains and naval architects and with experts in gunnery and explosives, in mining and quarrying, in watchmaking, coinage, astronomy, undertaking, and the constitutional relations between Church and State. And in Vienna he applied himself with such success to observing the dignified protocol of the Imperial Court that several ambassadors there spoke of his "delicate and polished manners," and one of them commented that "here he appears quite unlike the descriptions of other courts and far more civilized, intelligent, with excellent manners, and modest."*

But underneath his veneer of civilized manners the Czar of Muscovy was "the same weak woman still." Six weeks after he left Vienna he was back in Moscow where on the morning after his arrival he assembled the chief ministers, boyars, generals, and church dignitaries, and with a large pair of scissors proceeded to cut off their beards. With unerring intuition he recognised the beard as a symbol of Russian backwardness, and in his scissors he intended them to recognise a symbol of the ruthless manner in which he proposed to deal with it.

This incident in the life of Peter the Great prompts us to look again at the incident in the life of Alcibiades when he cut off his dog's tail, and to ask whether Plutarch has given us the whole truth about it or whether there was some deeper significance behind that seemingly senseless action. Can we really believe that Alcibiades, the friend of Socrates, committed that barbarous act of vandalism simply in order to secure notoriety for himself, that is to say, in order to acquire a bad reputation as a vandal? Or did it happen rather differently, perhaps like this?

It is late at night. A drinking party is in progress at Alcibiades' house and they are discussing their favourite topic - religion. Socrates has been provoking the guests into giving

* I. Gray. loc. cit. p. 130.

views on the uselessness of the church in the modern state and the harm done by its influence as a backward-looking force that is hindering progress towards a rational approach to the world's problems. The host, half drunk, is in hearty agreement and forcefully declares that he would like to abolish organised religion entirely.

A young man intervenes here in defence of religion, which he compares to Alcibiades' dog's magnificent tail. "It may be useless and backward-facing", he says. "But you've got to admit that it's an essential part of the animal and very ornamental. You can't just cut it off."

"Oh, can't I," says Alcibiades, in a sudden rage at being contradicted. "Just you watch." Whereat he seizes a carving knife and with one blow he severs the dog's tail from its body.

Next day he is ashamed of this atrocious act and wishes he could keep it secret; but the news leaks out. A notorious gossip calls to ask why he did it. "Why did I do it?" he retorts angrily, "I'll tell you why. I did it just in order to give nosey bastards like you something to talk about."

Peter's cutting off of his ministers' beards was followed up by a ukase ordering Russians to shave, or, as an alternative, to pay a tax graded according to their social status. This was a direct challenge to the authority of the Orthodox Church. "The Saviour himself and his apostles wore beards," said the Patriarch. "To shave one's beard is not only a dishonour, it is a mortal sin." Fearful of the possible consequences in the next world, many Russian citizens preferred to pay the tax, but some who found the tax too heavy shaved their beards but continued to carry them about on their persons, so that body and beard could be buried together and enable them to satisfy at least one of the conditions for entry into Heaven.

Peter next addressed himself to an inquiry into a revolt of the *streltsi* which had taken place in his absence. He had fourteen torture-chambers prepared at his country residence and personally supervised the interrogation under torture, and the execution in the most barbarous fashion, of over 800 men. Their bodies were left lying in the Red Square or hanging from the Kremlin walls throughout the winter as a warning to others.

The revolt for which this terrible punishment was meted out was a feeble affair which had never seriously threatened the Czar's position. The principal ringleaders, to the number of 130, had already been executed before his return. Undoubtedly the dominating motive behind Peter's cruelty was revenge for the injury that the *streltsi* had done him sixteen years before. Despite his profession of Christianity, he had not learned how to forgive; he was still the same revengeful Alcibiades.

Nor had his religion cured him of deceitfulness in dealings with his enemies. Just as he had tricked the Spartan envoys in 421 B.C., so he tricked the envoys of Charles XII of Sweden in A.D. 1700 when they came to him seeking an assurance of his friendship. He gave them, or so they believed, the assurance they sought: "you cannot think that I would begin an unjust war against the King of Sweden and break an eternal peace which I have just promised to preserve," he wrote to the Swedish representative at the very moment when he was plotting with the King of Denmark and the Elector of Saxony to launch an unprovoked attack on territory then in Swedish possession. Whilst he deceived the Swedes, what he said was literally true: they could not think that he would do what in fact he was intending to do.

Of Alcibiades' sexual activities we do not know enough to be able to make a judicious comparison with those of Peter the Great. Popular rumours, which are all that the historian whether ancient or modern usually has to go on in these matters, are notoriously unreliable. It was said that Alcibiades was attracted to both sexes and freely indulged in homosexual as well as heterosexual behaviour. He married an heiress who soon left him, according to Plutarch, because of his frequent infidelities and debaucheries; but he took her back by force and she remained with him until she died not long after. In Sparta he seduced the wife of King Agis. Finally, at the time of his death he was living with a mistress, Timandra, who had borne him a daughter and who appears to have been devoted to him, for she wrapped his body in her own robes and gave him an honourable burial.

This meagre record of Alcibiades' love life accords well enough with what we know of Peter's. The Czar's first marriage to the daughter of a conservative Muscovite family took place when he was not yet seventeen. The girl was not of his own choosing and the marriage was a failure. She bore him a son and heir, who was a cruel disappointment to him. After nine years Peter sent her away to end her days in a nunnery.

That sexual activities took place during the drunken orgies that Peter enjoyed cannot be doubted, and throughout his life he is known to have had many mistresses. But that is not to say that he was a libertine. On the contrary, he was by nature monogamous.*

* There is an instructive contrast between the life of Peter the Great and that of his fellow ruler and ally Augustus II "the Strong", Elector of Saxony and King of Poland. The two men were almost the same age, inherited the same tremendously powerful physique, the same attractiveness to women, and the same natural propensity towards licentious behaviour, and both enjoyed absolute power within their realms. But whereas Peter never let a love affair interfere with his work but was always ready to direct the full force of his vitality to overcoming the immense difficulties which he encountered in his reforms at home and his campaigns abroad, Augustus II regularly put pleasure before duty, dissipated his strength with women, and was said to have fathered over three hundred illegitimate children. The consequences were predictable. Peter developed, or at least retained, the courage, tenacity, and strength of intellect with which he was endowed at birth, and became the founder of a mighty empire; Augustus became cowardly, indolent, treacherous and weak-minded, lost all his dominions, and only regained his throne in the end thanks to Peter's magnanimity.

The abiding light of Peter's love life was his second wife Catherine I, a kindly, generous, good-natured woman of humble origin with whom he lived in close companionship for over twenty years and who was with him when he died. It is pleasing to think that in the happiness that Catherine shared with Peter over his victories and achievements, the selfless devotion with which Timandra had shared the exile and persecution of Alcibiades received its just reward.

Justice, too, but of a sterner kind, was apparently meted out to Alcibiades himself in his next incarnation. Let us consider the crimes of which he was accused.

The guying of the Mysteries was hardly more than a harmless prank. It was done secretly in private houses, and would have offended no one if the secret had been kept. The real offence lay not in the act itself but in the malicious reporting of it by jealous informers.

The mutilation of the Hermae however, was different. That was an act of vandalism that was plain for all to see. It had ruined many irreplaceable antiquities, was deeply offensive to many godfearing citizens, and the damage done could never be repaired.

These Hermae, or 'herms', were square stone pillars which originally stood dotted about the countryside in Attica (and nowhere else in Greece), having been set up in very ancient times as markers to mark the boundaries of farms and villages. They had two anthropomorphic features: The top of each herm was a sculpted head of the god Hermes, and from the middle of the front face of the pillar there projected the image of an erect phallus. On account of these features the herms were regarded as sacred icons which not merely represented, but somehow actually embodied, the divine life force, bestowing virility on men and fertility on women and on herds and crops.

An Attic Herm depicted on a plate. 5th Century B.C.

For these reasons they had been brought in from the country by rich city-dwellers and now stood outside houses and temples in the streets of Athens to bestow their much desired blessings on the inmates.

Though the historians were too delicate to say so explicitly, it is clear from a reference in a play by Aristophanes that the gravamen of the crime that was committed by the mutilators of the herms lay in their knocking off these projecting members. Who the culprits were was never established. Opinion at the time, and ever since, was divided between those who believed that the crime was part of a conspiracy with a sinister political objective, and those who regarded it as an impromptu work of wanton vandalism carried out by a group of drunken revellers.

There is no reliable evidence to prove either opinion right, so we are left to choose between them on the basis of which of the two appears the more probable. This is a question of personal choice, and I have no hesitation in choosing the drunken revel theory.* There is good evidence that Alcibiades played the leading part in the mockery of the Mysteries, and the mutilation of the herms was all of a piece with that burlesque in that it was manifestly aimed not at any political objective but at vilifying certain popular religious superstitions. It was also in keeping with Alcibiades' known propensity

* It was suggested that the mutilators were a group of Corinthians who were anxious to delay the sailing of the Athenian fleet against their colony in Syracuse. Another idea was that there was a plot by Alcibiades and his friends to overthrow the democracy and replace it with an oligarchy. Neither of these theories is credible. In neither case was there the smallest prospect of the alleged objective being achieved; nor was there evidence that any attempt was made to follow up the initial shock of the mutilations with a political coup.

towards heavy drinking, which often led to sudden rages and acts of violence. It seems to me highly probable that the young admiral-designate may have celebrated his impending departure for Sicily with a wild carouse that ended by his gang of inebriated young sparks roaming the streets in the small hours, giving vent to their energies by bashing the stone erections which *they* regarded as obscene but which sober people of the older generation more properly venerated as holy.

I am fortified in this opinion by knowing how Peter the Great met his death. In November 1724, in his fifty-third year, Peter was taken ill with a disease of the urinary tract. The malady worsened progressively until on January 20 a complete blockage made it impossible for him to pass water. From then on he was constantly in terrible agony. A short relief was gained when a surgeon carried out the painful operation of perforation of the bladder; but gangrene set in and the pain intensified. For all his immense strength and fortitude Peter was over-whelmed by suffering and was heard to murmur "I can't take any more." But he lingered on in agony till death at last released him on January 28, 1725.

Alcibiades eluded human justice when he defied the summons to appear before the judges in Athens in 415 B.C. But did he escape from justice altogether? Who can tell in what mysterious ways the avenging arm of divine justice may accomplish its end when a guilty but unpunished psyche returns to earth in a new incarnation? Where is the doctor who can diagnose some ailment or deformity as the consequence of some misdeed, the memory of which lay heavy on the patient's conscience as he departed from a former life?

Chapter Four
TWO INTO ONE

*Aeschylus (525 - 456 B.C.) + Aristophanes (448 - 385 B.C.)
= Shakespeare (A.D. 1564 - 1616)*

In a lecture delivered at the Royal Institution in London on May 29 1953, Sir John Sheppard, then Provost of King's College Cambridge, and formerly Professor of Greek at that University, demonstrated the extraordinary similarity of the two mind patterns that created the *Agamemnon* of Aeschylus and Shakespeare's *Macbeth*. The similarity is the more remarkable because the fatalistic attitude of the pagan religion with its prevailing ideas of fate and nemesis which formed the background of Greek tragedy was quite alien to the robust belief in the sovereignty of the individual that was inspired by Protestant Christianity and pervaded the spiritual atmosphere of Elizabethan England. Moreover, Shakespeare, as Sheppard pointed out, was not a Classical scholar. He had "small Latin and less Greek."

Sheppard recalled the memory of two great teachers, the Aeschylean scholar Walter Headlam at Cambridge, and the Shakespearian scholar A.C. Bradley at Oxford. Just about the time when Headlam was explaining how the art of Aeschylus resembles that of Beethoven, and how themes and images are interwoven in the fabric of his drama like recurrent motifs in a classical symphony, Bradley was saying how Shakespeare's themes and images are used to suggest a kind of musical pattern, now of discord, now of harmony, between the world of nature and the passionate and tortured spirits of his heroes and his heroines. It was just then, too, that a third scholar, Churton Collins, ardently proclaimed his faith that Shakespeare was actually inspired by reading Aeschylus. This claim was scorned by the pundits, and Collins was likened by Sheppard to Don Quixote tilting at windmills, trying to prove the impossible. "All three of these scholars," said Sheppard, "gave us cause, for which we should be humbly thankful, to read Aeschylus and Shakespeare side by side, and so discover something of the glory that ensues when two great poets, for whatever reason, *think and feel and seem to see the truth alike.*"*

"For whatever reason." What better reason could there be than that the minds of the two great poet-dramatists were in fact one and the same mind in two different incarnations?

"Look at the first lines," Sheppard continued, quoting Headlam. "If you want to understand the play. They state the subject and announce motifs that will develop in the sequel." He went on to compare the watchman's prologue in the *Agamemnon* with the witches scene in the prelude of *Macbeth*. The themes are different but the composer's skill with which the motifs are interwoven and developed is the same. The watchman is on the roof of Agamemnon's palace in Mycenae watching for the beacon signal that will announce that Troy has fallen. The first lines of the prologue state the subject: a prayer for deliverance from evil. The same prayer is repeated at the end of his first paragraph with a more passionate appeal, a far more sinister effect, because at the centre of the paragraph there has been mention of a woman, manlike, sanguine, masterful, who dominates the house. We know it is Clytemnestra and we know she means to kill her husband.

---

* This and subsequent quotations are taken from a lecture on *Agamemnon and Macbeth* by Sir John T. Sheppard, Litt.D.,LL.D., Provost of King's College, Cambridge, reported in the Proceedings of the Royal Institution of Great Britain, Vol. XXXV Part III, No.160, 1953.

The watchman sees the beacon .... With a significant break of rhythm he shouts -

> Ho there, within!
> A clear call that to Agamemnon's wife
> To rise with instant pious Hallelujah
> And greet this light which tells us Troy is ours."

Evil likewise is the subject of *Macbeth*, introduced in the witches prelude. After the first stanza which begins and ends with weather, there is a break of rhythm at the mention of the man who is going to murder his king.

> *First Witch*: Where the place.
> *Second Witch*: Upon the heath
> There to meet with Macbeth.

The final couplet,

> Fair is foul and foul is fair
> Hover through the fog and filthy air

completes the pattern, returning to the weather theme, but with a difference. Fair foul, foul fair, is a dominant notion in Greek tragedy ....

"This sort of formal patterning is Greek in origin. There are many instances in Homer .... But in drama Aeschylus, adopting this same formula to his dramatic purpose, comes closest to the use that Shakespeare makes of it throughout *Macbeth*."

A similar interweaving of the themes of sleep and dreams, dreams and sleep, occurs both in the *Agamemnon* and in *Macbeth*.

Sheppard did not dwell on the obvious parallel between the masterful murderesses Clytemnestra and Lady Macbeth.

He chose rather to point out the less obvious similarities between Aeschylus' Furies and Shakespeare's Witches.

He quoted the latter:

> I will drain him dry as hay ...
> He shall dwindle, peak and pine.

and compared it with Aeschylus -

> Who thrives by sin, his luck is hazardous,
> The tide turns. The dark Furies claim their prey.
> He dwindles, wanes, fades out, a shadow among
> shadows, where no help remains.

(Ag. 467 ff).)

We cannot for a moment think that Shakespeare could read Aeschylus as Headlam did. The fact remains that these weird sisters are significant for us and for his tragedy because they have upon them something of a mystical inheritance from Aeschylean Furies, following the trail 'fast as a ship in wingless flight' (Eum. 250), and chanting, when they find their prey, the spell

> That wastes and warps and withers, till the mind,
> Distracted, helpless, blind,
> Runs mad, and the heart breaks. It is the spell
> That binds the will, the Furies chant of Hell.

(Eum. 330 ff.)

That is what happens to Macbeth, not to his body but to his soul, and for him, after the frightful climax of his conjuration of the witches (IV 1.58-60), which itself is the sequel to his wife's appalling prayer, 'You spirits that attend on mortal thoughts ... unsex me here,' and after the massacre of the children, the last crowning infamy, nothing remains.

Life has become, for him, 'a tale told by an idiot, signifying nothing.'

The last of the above quotations from Aeschylus are taken not from the *Agamemnon* but from the third play of the Oresteia trilogy, the *Eumenides*. In this play Agamemnon's son Orestes, having on the orders of Apollo avenged his father by murdering Clytemnestra, is pursued by the Furies for the crime of matricide and seeks refuge in Athens where an Athenian court of justice tries him. The court being equally divided, the goddess Athena gives her casting vote on the side of mercy.

This episode of the trial of Orestes is not taken from orthodox Greek mythology but was an invention of the dramatist. In it we see the expression of an important trait in Aeschylus' character - his intense patriotism. In his earlier play the *Persae* he glorified Athens as the bastion of freedom - he had himself fought as a private soldier at Marathon - and now in the *Eumenides* he portrays his beloved city as the home of justice and mercy, divinely blessed. The same motif is developed and enlarged in the historical plays in which Shakespeare glorified his native England.

> "This royal throne of kings, this scepter'd isle,
> This earth of majesty, this seat of Mars,
> This other Eden, demi-Paradise ....
> This happy breed of men, this little world,
> This precious stone set in the silver sea ....
> This blessed plot, this earth, this realm, this England."*

Of the ninety plays which Aeschylus was reputed to have written, only seven survive in their entirety. These, however, are enough to enable us to confirm the judgement of his

* *King Richard II*, II. 1.40

46

contemporaries by which he was exalted into a class by himself, towering high above all other dramatists. By a decree of the Athenian Assembly passed soon after his death, the plays of Aeschylus were given the unique honour of being allowed to be staged posthumously at the annual festival of the Dionysia.

Aeschylus was a great innovator, and on account of his innovations he is regarded as the founder of Greek drama.

He turned what was till then a religious ritual into a play by introducing more characters and by elevating the dialogue between them into a position of dominance over the choruses. In the *Persae*, one of his characters is a ghost - a device which Shakespeare used with powerful dramatic effect in *Hamlet*.

An actor himself, like Shakespeare, Aeschylus' genius as a master of the stage was as many-sided as it was original and profound. The power and grandeur of his tragic themes, the nobility of his characters and the unbearable strains by which they are tormented, the rich poetic imagery of his language, the grandiloquent diction that he uses to cram a wealth of meaning into a few close-set words and teeming compounds often of his own invention - all these are qualities in which the plays of Aeschylus are unexcelled in ancient drama.

These qualities are all developed to the full in Shakespeare's tragedies. But Shakespeare has one outstanding quality that is wholly lacking in Aeschylus - humour. The Greek tragedian wrote no comedies, and we look in vain for a porter or a gravedigger to relieve the awful tensions of his tragedies. The seriousness of his nature is clearly reflected in his portrait. The deep-set eyes and furrowed brow, the drooping moustache and tousled beard all betray the profound solemnity of his brooding thoughts. In Shakespeare, on the other hand, the same oval high-domed countenance is lightened by an up-turned moustache and (in his later portraits) a neatly pointed beard; the furrows are smoothed out, and the expression is one of

AESCHYLUS
(525 - 456 B.C.)

SHAKESPEARE
(1564 - 1616)

calm contemplation in which the serious is evenly balanced by the gay.

Perhaps the clue to this transformation is to be found in the character of Sir John Falstaff, the jovial squire and companion of young Henry V, who symbolizes the full-blooded rollicking bawdy humour of Shakespeare's England together with the weaknesses of her people's character. Falstaff's prototype is surely Demus, the fat genial citizen who symbolizes both the good nature and the vacillating inconstancy of the Athenian people in the *Knights* of Aristophanes.

Aristophanes, the comic poet who enlivened war-torn Athens with his sparkling comedies was, like Aeschylus, a fervent patriot. But the city that he loved so passionately was not the floundering Athens of his own day, the city of Socrates and the sophists and their new morality, and of iconoclasts like Euripides and Alcibiades, but the heroic Athens of yesterday, the Athens of the Persian Wars and of Pericles the Olympian, the Thunderer at whose voice all Hellas trembled. The two cities were as different from one another as the postwar England of today is different from the England of Queen Victoria. Aristophanes was at heart a Victorian, a die-hard conservative and a believer in the old religion. Above all, he was a profound admirer of Aeschylus, whom he represents in the *Frogs* as the victor in a contest of wits with Euripides, the Bernard Shaw of ancient Greece.

Although Aeschylus had already been dead some years before Aristophanes was born, that need not be a bar to the two men's personalities coming together somewhere in the expanses of that region which is inhabited by souls in transit between lives. Admiration is a force of attraction that would combine with the comic poet's past-directed mental orientation to send his departed soul hastening in the direction of his hero, whilst the complementary nature of the two men's talents would ensure that a harmonious inter-penetration took place when finally their personalities came into contact. Thus, we may reasonably surmise that the dearest wish of Aristophanes was fulfilled in a manner beyond his wildest dreams when he not only encountered but was spiritually and physically united with his hero Aeschylus, and the two poets were born again as one, to create the genius of the world's greatest master of tragedy *and* comedy, the genius of Shakespeare.

Chapter Five
ONE INTO TWO

Plato (428 - 328 B.C.) = Hobbes (A.D. 1588 - 1679)
+ Descartes (A.D. 1596 - 1650)

The name of Plato looms so large in the history of ideas that at times it has almost seemed to be synonymous with the name Philosophy itself. No other thinker except Aristotle has ever exercised so profound and far-reaching an influence on the development of rational thought. When, therefore, one looks through the names of European philosophers of more recent times amongst whom we would expect to find the mind of Plato reincarnate, one is puzzled by the absence of any giant of corresponding stature.

This could be due to the changed environment resulting from the growth in stature of many smaller minds during the intervening period, so that those who stood out as giants in former lives no longer overtop their contemporaries by the same margin as before. Or it could be that Plato's intellect had already reached the limit of spiritual length, breadth and depth that can feasibly be accommodated within the physical limitations of a human skull and that, like a raindrop which has grown so big that the cohesive force of its surface tension is no longer strong enough to resist the disruptive forces that are generated by the passage of its bulk through the air, his spirit was split in half and returned to earth as two distinct human beings.

Internal tensions are bound to arise in a great thinker's mind on account of the dimensional conflict that springs from his being a spiritual force in a material world. The four-dimensional double spin of the psyche is trying to do two things at once: to establish harmonious relations with its environment, and to maintain order within itself. The former effort requires a strong "tangential" force on the outer surface, moulding that surface to the shape of its environment and smoothing out roughnesses in the environment itself; the latter requires a strong "radial" force to maintain internal cohesion and to prevent the tangential force from dissipating itself in too great extension. These two order-creating forces are thus in tension, the effect of the one being centrifugal, that of the other centripetal.

The physical result of this tension is manifest in the crinkles in the surface of the brain. The force that would cause the surface to expand is held in check by the radial force that maintains internal harmony by pulling the surface in towards the centre. Let us now see how this tension was manifest in the mental activity of the world's greatest thinker.

Plato was born in Athens of aristocratic parents one year after the death of Pericles. His real name was Aristocles; "Plato" was a nickname meaning "broad" given to him on account of the great breadth of his brow. He was brought up during the Peloponnesian War and spent his first years of manhood fighting, probably as a cavalry officer. He was twenty-four when his country was finally defeated and its constitution overthrown. Five years later Socrates, whom he knew well and admired above all other men, was put to death for asking questions.

A man of Plato's birth, wealth, and education would normally have made his career in politics, but these events, coupled with a naturally shy disposition and the fact that his voice was thin and feeble, set him against public life. He travelled to Sicily and South Italy where he came across the remnants of the Pythagorean movement, perhaps visited Egypt, and then returned to Athens where, in the grove sacred to the Attic hero Academus, he founded his *Academy*, the western world's first University. There he spent most of the rest of his life teaching his pupils by lectures and seminars after the manner of Pythagoras. The principal subject which he taught was mathematics, and it was said that the inscription over the gate of his Academy read: "Let no one enter here who cannot do geometry."

It is my contention that Plato was a methematician who had discovered for himself the secret of Pythagoras. He understood the geometry of the true Pythagorean *tetractys*, but he never divulged it. He hinted darkly at his secret knowledge, wrote in riddles and parables, and left a number of cryptic clues as to their meaning; but even to those who were closest to him he never revealed the true foundation on which his philosophy rested. He thus led a double life, in which the inner workings of his mind were in perpetual tension with the outer semblance of his teaching. This tension was reflected in a conflict of aim. Having, like Pythagoras, seen the Truth, he wanted like him to build a perfect society. But the world was not yet ready. He was like an architect who sees a vision of a marble palace, but not enough marble to build it has yet been quarried and the only materials at his disposal are mud bricks. The men and women Plato had available as materials from which to construct his ideal society were mostly ignorant and stupid. What should he do? Should he spend his life trying to educate them in the way of enlightenment, or should he take them as they were and design the best society he could from them - a society which could only be very far from perfect?

The first part of his life Plato devoted to the realisation of the former aim, which coincided with his desire to build a logically coherent system of thought compounded from the scientific approach of Socrates and the mathematical approach of Pythagoras. In his earlier works, therefore, he discoursed on truth, beauty, and goodness, on the pursuit of knowledge, on love, and on the immortality of the soul. In the *Republic* he comes very near to an ideal reconciliation of his two aims. But in his last work, the *Laws*, he seems to have accepted the incorrigibility of human nature and resigns himself to devising a political system that will, so to speak, make the best of a bad job.

In the latter years of his life, Plato made two visits to Sicily in the vain hope that by his personal influence on Dionysius II, the young ruler of Syracuse, he might influence the course of at least one important polity in the direction of justice and reason. But his mission was a miserable failure. When he died at the age of eighty it must have been in the knowledge that his aim of effecting some immediate improvement in the way men govern their affairs had not been fulfilled; all he had left was a hope that out of the darkness where he could not see some other hand would pick up the torch of the Knowledge of Mathematical Truth that he was now forced to let fall, and would carry his work to a more successful fulfilment.

At the end of the 16th century of our era two philosophers were born who between them covered the vast range of Plato's thought. Thomas Hobbes was born at Malmesbury, in the west of England on April 5th 1588; René Descartes was born at La Haye (Touraine) in the west of France on March 31st 1596. Their lives and works are such as to suggest that at some time between the fourth century B.C. and the sixteenth century A.D. Plato's soul became divided, and one half was reincarnate in the person of Hobbes, the other in Descartes.

PLATO
(428 - 328 B.C.)

THOMAS HOBBES
(1588 - 1679)

RENÉ DESCARTES
(1596 - 1650)

The political, pragmatic, and more typically English side of his genius was attracted to England, while the mathematical, logical, more strictly philosophical, and more typically French side was attracted to France.

The differences in the two sets of qualities are reflected in the difference in the shapes of the two men's heads. The nose, mouth and chin are similar in both faces, but Hobbes' head is big and his forehead high, denoting a high ratio of tangential to radial force in his brain, i.e. an excess of pragmatism over logic, while Descartes' head is small and his forehead low and flat, indicating a mind in which the capacity for logical reasoning is higher than its practical commonsense.

Thomas Hobbes was the son of a country vicar. Though not born an aristocrat, he was well educated and found himself instinctively at home with the aristocracy. After leaving Oxford he became private tutor to William Cavendish, afterwards second Earl of Devonshire, and spent a large part of the rest of his life at Chatsworth, the palatial mansion which is still the home of the Dukes of Devonshire.

He was of a shy disposition, and for the first forty years of his life he achieved nothing of note, though he travelled through Europe and mixed with the most distinguished intellects of the day. He was particularly attracted to the intellectual milieu of Paris, where he became attached to the group of thinkers that gathered round Mersenne, the friend of Descartes.

What has been called Hobbes's "philosophic awakening" came when he was about forty-two, and was due to his picking up a copy of Euclid's *Geometry*. It was borne in upon him that the causes of all phenomena were to be found in spatio-temporal relations or in diversity of motion, whence it followed that the Ultimate Cause of everything must be looked for in geometry. Thereafter he spent much time working at geometry, but he was a poor mathematician and his excursions into that field brought him no credit.

Hobbes's fame rests on his achievements in the realm of political theory, and in particular on his masterpiece, the *Leviathan* which was published in 1651 when he was sixty-three. That book is a systematic attempt to lay down principles for the organisation of an ideal state based on reason, regardless of historical associations. Like Plato's ideal *Republic*, Hobbes's *Leviathan* is governed by an authoritarian aristocracy, a specially selected group of men who are educated in moral philosophy and devote themselves to promoting the spiritual as well as the material well-being of the people. The latter, however, are not slaves, for they retain their individuality and only lose those freedoms which are incompatible with the rational ordering of public affairs.

Hobbes's style is imaginative, "not merely on account of the subtle imagery that fills his pages, nor only because it requires imagination to make a system. His imagination appears also as the power to create a myth. The *Leviathan* is a myth, the transposition of an abstract argument into the world of the imagination. In it we are made aware at a glance of the fixed and simple centre of a universe of complex and changing relationships. The argument may not be the better for this transposition, and what it gains in vividness it may pay for in illusion. But it is an accomplishment of art that Hobbes, in the history of political philosophy shares only with Plato."*

But despite the vast amount of energy that Hobbes expended on this design of an ideal political system, he was pessimistic about its chances of ever being put into practice. Perhaps he recalled, subconsciously, his unhappy experience with Dionysius. At the end of the second part of the *Leviathan* he wrote as follows.

* Michael Oakeshott in his Introduction to the *Leviathan* of Thomas Hobbes published by Basil Blackwell, Oxford, p.xviii.

"And now, considering how different this doctrine is from the practice of the greatest part of the world, especially of these western parts, that have received their moral learning from Rome and Athens; and how much depth of moral philosophy is required in them that have the administration of the sovereign power; I am at the point of believing this my labour as useless as the commonwealth of Plato. For he also is of opinion that it is impossible for the disorders of state, and change of governments by civil war, ever to be taken away, till sovereigns be philosophers."

With a struggle, however, he overcomes his pessimism and goes on to hope that one day his book will fall into the hands of a sovereign who will understand it and "convert this truth of speculation into the utility of practice."

Hobbes wrote his autobiography at the age of eighty-four and died in his ninety-second year. The personal characteristics which he shared with Plato were many: enormous mental energy, scepticism and independence of mind, absolute confidence in the rightness of his opinions, disputatiousness, urbanity, an ironical wit, a shrewd sagacity, and a passion for systematising.

If the practical and political side of Plato's psyche - the side that was uppermost in the *latter* part of his life - was reincarnate in Hobbes, it is undoubtedly in René Descartes, "the founder of modern philosophy,"* that we find resurrected the mathematical and spiritual genius which shone with such brilliance in the *earlier* part of Plato's life.

* Bertrand Russell in the *Wisdom of the West* edited by Paul Foulkes; MacDonald, London, 1959, p.194.

Descartes' family belonged to the lesser nobility, his father being a councillor of the parliament of Brittany. Descartes thus had an excellent opportunity to embark on a political career if he had wished to. His brother was a lawyer, and he graduated in law himself, but he had no interest in law or politics. He was of a shy and retiring disposition, and his voice was thin and feeble. After completing his education at a Jesuit College and at the University of Poitiers, he devoted himself for a while - surprisingly, until one remembers Plato's early life - to riding and fencing; and when the Thrity Years War broke out in 1618, being then twenty-two, he went to Holland to enlist as a soldier.

In the following year Descartes found himself quartered in a village near Ulm on the Danube, where he had a spiritual experience of the nature of a divine revelation that affected his whole life. He had a series of dreams which he interpreted as meaning that he was destined to be the founder of a new scientific philosophy. He was to unite science and mathematics, or rather to discover the derivation of science from mathematics, but he was to keep the discovery to himself. Science was to be to him as a chaste wife whom no other man should approach. He was to be like an actor in a mask, deliberately concealing his true knowledge from the world.

Religion was to play a purely passive part in this scheme. In the first of his dreams Descartes had seemed to be lame, trying to walk up a road to a church but deflected by a wind and blown against the side of the church where he had to shelter. Throughout his life Descartes scrupulously avoided religious controversy. He was influenced by the trial of Galileo (1633) as strongly as Plato had been influenced by the trial of Socrates, and on account of it he withheld the publication of certain of his works that he feared might give offence to the ecclesiastical authorities. (This did not, however, save his books from being subsequently placed on the Index on account of the inherent scepticism of his method of enquiry).

In Ulm he was attracted to the beliefs of the Rosicrucians, an occult society which claimed to possess secret knowledge and whose origin may be traceable back to the original religion of Pythagoras. But there is no evidence that Descartes actually became a Rosicrucian, as some have held.

In 1624, in acknowledgement of his revelation, he went on a pilgrimage to the shrine of Our Lady of Loretto.

Like Plato and Hobbes, Descartes held himself aloof from other thinkers and pursued his own thoughts independently. When, after further travels, he settled in Paris, he found the presence there of many other brilliant minds gathered round his friend Mersenne a distracting rather than a stimulating influence. At a meeting of philosophers in 1629 Chardoux maintained that there was no certainty in science, but all scientific conclusions were based on probability. Descartes intervened to contradict this assertion. He said that science was based on certainty, and he hinted, Plato-like, that he alone knew the secret of that certainty. He was promptly challenged to explain the secret in writing, but he declined. It was probably this experience more than any other that prompted him to leave Paris in search of a more tranquil environment, which he found in Holland.

Descartes' great contributions to philosophy were just what might be expected if our hypothesis regarding his psychogenic genealogy is right. His three great ideas were: first, the supreme importance of seeking knowledge of the truth, and of adopting the right method of logical analysis and deduction for arriving at that knowledge; secondly, the unity of science and mathematics; and thirdly, the dualism of mind and matter and the supremacy of mind over matter. He also insisted, in common with his Christian co-religionists, on the immortality of the soul, and he wrote a discourse on Love. In all these works Descartes' philosophy closely parallels that of Plato. Above all Descartes, like Plato, sensed that the road to Truth led through geometry. He even insisted on his servants learning the elements of Euclid.

Like Plato, too, Descartes spoke in riddles. He pursued a deliberate policy of secrecy and mystification. His great work on *Geometry* - the most important of all his contributions to western thought, from which is derived our system of algebraic expression in terms of "Cartesian coordinates" (graphs) - was purposefully written in a style so difficult and obscure that only a few men should be able to understand it. But whereas Plato, according to my submission, actually possessed the knowledge of the Pythagorean secret of reincarnation, it is evident that Descartes did not. He looked to the science of medicine to find a cure for senescence and to solve the problem of old age.

It is interesting to note that the only contact that existed between Descartes and Hobbes arose from a disagreement. The English philosopher with his more practical outlook objected to the pure metaphysics of Descartes' famous proposition "I think, therefore I exist", and wrote a treatise to refute it. The quarrel was, I suggest, but a continuation of the conflict in Plato's mind. It was also symptomatic of the age-long quarrel between the muddy but fertile pragmatism of the English and the clear but sterile logic of the French - a conflict that has since been repeated a thousand times on the battlefield of war and in the international conference room. But though the two men disagreed in their ways of thinking, they shared together a common aversion to the Germanic Aristotle, whose pulverizing philosophy Hobbes stigmatised as "vain", while Descartes claimed to have confounded it in his *Discourse on Method.*

Descartes died when he was fifty-four, the age at which Hobbes was just embarking on the most productive period of his career. Both men in their later years accepted appointments as instructors in royal households, just as Plato had done in Sicily. Hobbes became tutor to Charles, Prince of Wales, in exile in Paris, and Descartes to Christina, Queen of Sweden. It was the rigours of the Swedish winter and the Queen's insistence that the philosopher must abandon his usual habit of staying in bed till mid-day, in order to instruct her at 5 a.m., that was reputed to have brought on the illness of which he died. His last work was to draft a statute for the establishment of an Academy of Science in Stockholm. As he worked on the founding of that Academy, did he perchance experience that feeling that "this has all happened before"?

Chapter Six
OTHER GREEKS

The ten lives that I have discussed in some detail in the preceding chapters have, I hope, served to illustrate the main features of the reincarnation mechanism defined in the first chapter. The lives were selected with that end in view. In the present section I shall deal more briefly with a number of other lives in order to illustrate some of the side effects of the theory, and to fill in gaps in the historical sequence so as to make it possible to arrive at some conclusion regarding the changing shape of the western world's spiritual orbit.

Continuing first the story of Greek philosophy, we come to ARISTOTLE (B.C. 384 - 322), the Thracian polymath and universal genius, tutor to Alexander the Great and writer of text-books on physics, biology, phychology, logic, ethics, politics, poetry, and metaphysics.

If our picture of him is right, Aristotle was so eager to acquire fame for the brilliance of his own ideas that he was not willing to listen patiently to his master Plato; and in consequence he failed to pick up the clues that Plato dropped which would have told him where to look for the secret knowledge of Pythagoras. Though he must have studied mathematics at the Academy, he paid less attention to that subject than to any other, and he wrote a treatise in refutation of what he took to be the doctrines of the Pythagoreans. He founded the Lyceum in Athens, a rival school to the Academy, but after the death of Alexander he retired to Chalcis in Euboea, due north of Athens, where he died at the age of sixty-two.

There is only one star in the firmament of modern philosophers that shed such brilliant light on so many subjects as Aristotle. Gottfried Wilhelm LEIBNIZ (1646-1716) was born at Leipzig, the son of a university professor. He could read Latin and Greek by the time he was twelve, was writing theses on logic before he was fifteen, and thereafter devoted himself to the study of law, mathematics, history, religion, politics, psychology, science and philosophy, to all of which subjects he made not inconsiderable contributions. If we assume that Aristotle in retirement before he died regretted not having paid more attention to mathematics and, with characteristic fairness of mind, was conscience-stricken by the feeling that he had not done justice to the doctrines of Pythagoras, this would account for the fact that Leibniz concentrated a great deal of his attention on mathematics and his outstanding contribution to world thought was in that field, namely his invention of the differential and integral calculus. It would also perhaps explain why Leibniz based his metaphysical doctrine on a system of "monads" not unlike the basic units of the Pythagoreans.

Like Aristotle, Leibniz was eager to win renown as a thinker. But unlike the Greek, who lived and died enjoying fame and affluence under the patronage of kings, Leibniz died poor and miserably neglected by the world. No notice was taken of his death by the academy he had founded in Berlin, and the only mourner at his funeral was his secretary. "He was buried", said an eyewitness, "more like a robber than what he really was, the ornament of his country."

At this point, the reader is sure to ask: what about SOCRATES (B.C. 470-399)? Where shall we find that patient, gentle, enquiring soul returned to earth? What just reward was he accorded for the great injustice he received at the hands of the Athenians?

These questions are not easy to answer with any certainty. In his achievement, in his attitude to religion, and to some extent in facial features Socrates is resembled by Galileo Galilei

(1564-1642); whilst his introduction of a new scientific method of enquiry is more closely parallelled by the work of Francis Bacon (1561-1626). The date of birth of either of these philosophers would fit our time-scale, but the impetuous nature of the one and the worldly ambition of the other seem equally out of keeping with the character of Socrates as handed down to us by the ancients.

The person who seems to me most nearly to answer that description is CHARLES DARWIN (1809-1882). A kindly, modest soul, always more considerate of others than of himself and caring for truth above all things, Darwin's patient collection and meticulous examination of facts, his deep human sympathy, his unpretentiousness and gentle humour, and the fearless integrity with which he set out plainly and simply the truth as it was revealed to him regardless of how it might conflict with the Bible; all these recall the life and character of Socrates. The great difference in the climate of opinion between nineteenth century England and Athens of the fifth century B.C., coupled with the natural process of psychogenic development from one life to another, are sufficient to account for the fact that whereas Socrates' life was spent hacking a clearing in the primeval jungle of ignorance and superstition by asking questions, Darwin was able to sow the seeds of constructive thought in the field thus cleared and to reap the fruit of his work in the acclaim that he won for his theory of evolution by natural selection. The *Origin of Species* was the natural culmination of the Socratic search for knowledge.

Socrates was renowned for the ugliness of his face, but he never minded the jokes that were made about it. Vanity found no place in his nature. So we should expect to find him in his next life little changed in appearance. Darwin's features were not as ugly as, but bore a marked resemblance to, those of Socrates.

SOCRATES
(B.C. 470-399c)

DARWIN
(1809-1882)

By contrast, Darwin's matrimonial life was utterly different from that of the Greek. Socrates' wife Xantippe, according to the popular legend, was a woman of worldly ambition and of a disagreeable and unsympathetic character who had no use for her husband's philosophizing and was for ever nagging him for being content to live in poverty instead of getting on as other men did and making money. One day she ended a particularly stormy outburst by emptying a bucket of dirty water on his head; whereat the philosopher remarked: "... after thunder, comes the rain." No such quarrels marred the happiness of the Darwins' home. The Victorian scientist was comfortably endowed with inherited means, and his wife was an affectionate, unselfish, and sympathetic woman who looked after her ailing husband with loving care, denying herself many social pleasures that she would have enjoyed, in order to save him from fatigue.

The big difficulty in this diagnosis is the date. Socrates ought to have been reborn before Plato, in the sixteenth century. The explanation may be this. Socrates was a man of robust physique who carried his policy of self-control to the extreme. His mind was the master of his body to such an extent that he seemed to be oblivious to all normal physical pains and pleasures. He bore fatigues and discomforts that few other men could stand. Wearing the same rough clothing all the year round, he exposed himself to extremes of heat and cold without appearing to feel either, and went barefoot at all seasons even during a winter campaign in the snows of Thrace. When and what he ate and drank seemed to be questions of complete indifference to him. It would not be surprising if, in consequence, Socrates' maltreated and neglected body took revenge on him in his next life and he was born, as Darwin was, with feeble and delicate health, an easy prey to all manner of ailments. In the sixteenth century a sickly babe had little chance of surviving birth and infancy, and it could be that it was not until the nineteenth century that Socrates' soul, after repeated abortive attempts to come into the world, at last succeeded in being born with the help of improved medical care.

It may be remarked here that the orbital periods we have deduced for the souls of Aeschylus, Plato and Aristotle, and which we said should have been allowed for Socrates, are considerably shorter than those assumed for Pericles and Alcibiades. This is in accordance with the theory that men of thought return sooner than men of action.

This discrepancy may account for one of the curious facts of the Renaissance: that in the sixteenth century there appeared in Italy the most dazzling constellations of painters and sculptors that the world has ever seen, without a single states-man or soldier of more than mediocre calibre. After the defeat of the Persian invasions by the Greeks in B.C. 480 and 479, and the consequent lifting from the soul of Europe of the fear of Asian tyranny, there was a sudden bursting forth of new life in every field of human enterprise. In this flowering of genius, statesmen, thinkers, artists and poets all shone together in the tightly packed space of the Greek peninsular. But in death the souls of those great men fanned, out and when they returned to earth they appeared scattered over a wider area and a longer period of time. Here and there groups of like minds tended to adhere together, but they were separated from other groups in the general expansion of European civilization.

The artists evidently formed the most cohesive group and collected together in Rome, Florence, and the other great art schools of the Italian Renaissance. We would like to be able to identify at least the outstanding geniuses of ancient Greece in their Italian incarnations, but lack the material knowledge to do more than suggest the equation of PHIDIAS (B.C. 490-

432), reputedly the greatest of Greek sculptors, who excelled in his portrayal of divine majesty, with MICHELANGELO (1475-1564).

So far we have considered only examples of reincarnation after a full orbit, and have omitted the intermediate half-orbital lives for want of clear knowledge. Let us now consider a man of a very different character whom we may be able to recognise, albeit dimly, when reborn after a half-orbit in the Dark Ages.

ALEXANDER THE GREAT (B.C. 356-323) succeeded to the kingdom of Macedon at the age of twenty when his father Philip II was murdered, and set out two years later to conquer the Persian Empire. His invasion of Persia was an act of unprovoked aggression. He saw himself as a divinely inspired agent sent by Zeus to carry the light of Hellenic civilization into the furthest corners of the eastern world. In battle after battle he defeated the armies that were arrayed against him; he burned the palace of the Great King and exterminated his line; and he established Greek settlements, religion, and government from the Danube to the Indus and from Cyrene to Samarkand. The Macedonian Empire that Alexander the Great conquered was the mightiest empire yet seen on earth.

Alexander died in Babylon at the age of thirty-three, a European conqueror in the heart of Asia, far to the east of the centre of the western culture to which he belonged. Some seven or eight centuries later a lone figure can be discerned amid the shadows in the extreme west of what was then left of European civilization. In the fifth century A. D. the Romans withdrew from their province Britain, leaving the inhabitants to look after themselves as best they could. There was no organized machinery of government, and the undefended island became an easy prey to invading hordes from across the sea.

According to legend, ARTHUR was born at this time in the rocky fastness of Tintagel in remote Cornwall. Alexander was born the heir to a kingdon; Arthur, it seems, was a poor boy who was adopted by the lord of Tintagel. Elected as a young man to command what armies he could raise to defend his country and the Christian religion against the Saxon invaders, Arthur won battle after battle but found himself for ever out-numbered. Inch by inch his kingdom was wrenched from him and he was driven further and further west into the mountains of Wales as fresh waves of barbarians swarmed in to take the place of those who were slain. Finally he was slain himself, a victim of treachery, by one of his own generals.

If Alexander the Great was reincarnated in the person of King Arthur, then indeed was justice done. The prophecy that "he who takes the sword shall perish by the sword" was strikingly fulfilled; and in Arthur's death at the hand of Sir Mordred Alexander's cold-blooded murder of his general Parmenio was avenged. Two episodes may be mentioned as pointers to this diagnosis.

Soon after Alexander set foot in Asia he came to the Phrygian town of Gordium. Here in the temple of Zeus was a wagon, the yoke of which was bound to the pole by a strangely entwined knot. An ancient oracle had prophesied that whoever should loose the knot would conquer all Asia. Probably the knot was of the type that can be tied, after unravelling the strands of the two ends, in such a way that once it has been pulled tight it is *impossible* to undo. After one vain attempt to loose it, Alexander took his sword and with one stroke he cut the Gordian knot, thus establishing his claim to become the ruler of Asia.

Compare this story with that of the way in which Arthur established his claim to the kingship of England. In the greatest church in London there appeared by the high altar a great stone, in the middle of which was an anvil of steel. In the anvil was stuck a naked sword, and in letters of gold round the sword was written: "whoso pulleth out this sword of this stone and anvil is the rightful born King of England." Arthur, then a lad, was accompanying his guardian Sir Ector and his foster-brother Sir Kaye on their way to a jousting tournament when Sir Kaye realised he had forgotten to bring his sword. Arthur was sent back to fetch it, and reappeared shortly with his famous sword Excalibur, which he said he had pulled out of the stone without difficulty; whereat Sir Ector knelt before him as his future King.

If this story is true, it would appear that the Church was carrying out its historic function of appointing a king by means of its historic weapon: magic. There being no established line of kings in England, the position was like that which faced the high priest Samuel when he was compelled to appoint a king over Israel. The Church's problem was to find a man in whom a martial spirit was combined with high intelligence. The sword was fixed firmly in the anvil by means of a cunning mechanism and could only be released by pressing a hidden spring. Of the multitude of aspirants who tugged at the sword in vain Arthur, though only a lad, was the only one who had the wit to realise that there must be a catch somewhere. Given an opportunity to examine it when no one else was present, he found the catch and pulled the sword out without effort.

The character of Alexander the Great was full of inconsistencies. Plutarch describes him as "brave and pusillanimous, merciful and cruel, modest and vain, abstemious and luxurious, rational and superstitious, chivalrous and overbearing, politic and imprudent." If we make allowance for the fact that in the character of a hero who is known only through legend the good points tend to become exaggerated and the bad forgotten (the reverse with a villain), this description fits well enough the character of the legendary King Arthur; and if Arthur was in fact the reincarnation of the great world-conqueror, it is not surprising that, although historical records of the times he lived in are lacking, the memory of his deeds was never forgotten.

If Arthur's dying instruction to Sir Lancelot to throw his sword Excalibur into the lake meant that at last Alexander the Great had had enough of fighting and was ready to turn to peaceful pursuits in his next life, the same certainly was not true of that great imperialist, his father, PHILIP OF MACEDON (B. C. 382-336). Philip was murdered, like Julius Caesar, when he was on the point of setting out with his army to conquer the East. He had already conquered and unified under his strong control the quarrelsome states of Greece, but peace in the West could not be securely established until the threat of interference from the Persian Empire had been removed.

The motive that inspired Philip's conquests was not simply personal ambition or a mania for self-aggrandisement. It was the motive of the lone strong man, the masterful organiser who is born into a leaderless world of muddle and confusion, the man of decision who can see clearly, and who finds himself alone in a country of blind men. He wanted to see peace and order created out of disorder, and he knew that the only way it could be done was for him to take up his sword and organise the world himself.

The same strong arm, the same lone figure establishing unity out of confusion by the might of his sword, is discernible again in the European imperialism of CHARLEMAGNE

(A. D. 742-814), and again in NAPOLEON BONAPARTE (A.D. 1769-1821). Both those great emperors, having ordered their empires in the West, turned eastwards to remove the threat of invasion from that quarter. But Napoleon's Russian campaign ended in disaster, and before he died he saw his aspiration of a united Europe shattered beyond repair. One may speculate whether, if nation states were still to exist when his soul comes round again, and if war were then still an instrument of policy, he would wish to tread the same hard road over again.

We come now to the last of the ancient Greeks and the first of the historic kings of England.

At the beginning of the second century B. C. the city states of Greece were in much the same predicament as that in which the nation states of Europe find themselves today. The Greeks of that time were the lineal descendents of the great men who had lit the torch of Hellenic culture and blazed it forth over all the world; and they were unable to forget it. But the centres of power now lay elsewhere. After two wars in which the Romans, mindful of their Greek cultural heritage and defenders of freedom against tyranny, had come to the assistance of the other Greek states against the aggressions of their young north-eastern cousin, Macedonia - just as the Americans twice came to the assistance of the western European countries against the aggressions of Germany - the Macedonian power in Europe was permanently crushed; and the Greek states, with Macedon included, were left for a while in precarious enjoyment of their freedom, sandwiched between the growing might of Rome in the West and the massive power of the Seleucid Emperors who had inherited Alexander's conquests in the East.*

In these circumstances the only hope of independent survival for the Greek states lay in sinking their age-long differences and in forming a political union that would constitute a third power, strong enough to hold the balance between East and West. But Athens, to whom, as to England in post-war Europe, her sister states naturally looked for leadership, did not respond to the call. She had her gaze fixed far away on the vapour-trail of her vanished empire. And Sparta, whose dominant position in the Peloponnese corresponded with the position of France on the continent of Europe today, was ruled by a man** who thought that Sparta was still important.

So it was in the smaller states of the northern Peloponnese that the movement for unity took shape, and it was there that we find the only signs of long-sighted statesmanship in that dismal age. In Aratus of Sicyon, the founder of the Achaean League - the Benelux of those days - Greece produced a

---

* The two wars referred to were both fought against Philip V of Macedon. The first (B.C. 211-205) was inconclusive, the second (B.C. 200-194) was decisive. One other curious parallel with modern history may be noted: the second Macedonian War was immediately preceded by a cynical pact between Philip and the Seleucid Emperor Antiochus the Great for the partition of Egypt, just as the second German War was immediately preceded by a cynical pact between Germany and Russia for the partition of Poland.

** More precisely, two men in succession: Mechanidas, who was defeated and killed in battle by Philopoemen, and his successor Nabis. Both these kings of Sparta pursued a policy of trying to subject the whole of the Peloponnese to Spartan hegemony.

political genius, and in Philopoemen of Megalopolis a military genius, who between them nearly succeeded in uniting Hellas. But their efforts were brought to nought by the apathy of the people and by the short-sighted vainglory of their rulers. Neither governments nor people could see that in order to save their independence they had first to lose it. The Romans, in the end, had no alternative but to make Greece a Roman province.

It is with PHILOPOEMEN (B.C. 253-184), whom the Romans described as "the last of the Greeks", that we are here concerned. Though not a professional soldier (because Greek cities kept no standing armies) Philopoemen made a special study of the art of land warfare, and when not engaged in fighting at home he took service with armies abroad in order to study their methods. He was a man of great strength, courage, energy, and endurance, and a natural born leader of men. He was mainly responsible for the organisation, equipment, and training of the army of the Achaean League and three times led it to victory against Sparta. In an age of cynicism, corruption, and political ambition, he was remarkable for the simplicity of his style and his complete honesty.

His character is well illustrated by a story of Plutarch's. When, after the death of the Spartan King Nabis, Philopoemen at length succeeded in bringing Sparta temporarily into the Achaean League, the leading Spartans wished to express their gratitude for his leadership, and to secure his lasting friendship, by making him a present of Nabis's large personal fortune. But the envoy who was sent to make the gift was so impressed by the gravity of the general's discourse, the simplicity of his diet, and his integrity of manners, quite impregnable to the attacks and deceits of money, that he could not bring himself to mention the present. The same thing happened when the Spartans sent the envoy back a second time, and it was not till the third visit that, with much embarrassment, the envoy brought himself to explain why he had come. Philopoemen was pleased with the offer but went at once to Sparta and advised the people not to try to tempt good men with money who were already their friends, "but to buy and corrupt ill men who opposed their measures in council, that, thus silenced, they might give them less trouble."

Philopoemen's public life was spent in an unsuccessful uphill struggle to secure the unity of the Greek states in the Peloponnese and to defend their freedom against the two superpowers of Rome and Antioch. With this objective, he tried to get Sparta, Messene, and other southern states to join the Achaean League. But the weakness of the League lay in the fact that its members retained their several sovereignties and were consequently free to withdraw from it whenever they disapproved of the policies which the other members wished to pursue. When the Spartans, shortly after they had been persuaded, with great difficulty, to join, decided to withdraw again, Philopoemen became understandably exasperated. With his army from Megalopolis he marched against Sparta, demolished the city's walls, expropriated a large part of her territory, and finally destroyed the ancient constitution and discipline of Lycurgus, which he recognised as the fundamental obstacle to Sparta's merging her sovereignty in that of Hellas.

But this drastic treatment of the strongest state in the Peloponnese did not prevent others from following Sparta's example of threatening to break the unity of the Achaean League by withdrawal. Messene was the next. It was in fighting to bring that city back into the fold that Philopoemen lost his life.

The requirements of geometric symmetry would be fittingly met if the next life of "the last of the Greeks" were to be spent in a *successful* struggle to create a unified nation out of a number of independent sovereignties and to defend the freedom of his people, thus united, against foreign invaders. ALFRED THE GREAT (A.D. 848-900) may properly be called "the first of the English" because he liquidated the separate sovereignties of Wessex, Mercia, East Anglia, and Northumbria, and created from them the Kingdom of England. In the simplicity and integrity of his character he closely resembles Philopoemen, as also in his qualities as a soldier and organiser of an army. In the role of national leader both men attached the highest importance to the education, training, and discipline of youth.

Although Alfred was immune to bribery himself, he did not hesitate to use money to buy off the attacks of the Danes when it suited him to do so, thus following Philopoemen's advice "to buy and corrupt ill men, that, thus silenced, they might give less trouble."

In his work as a civil administrator, lawgiver, and organiser, Alfred was only exercising talents that he had acquired by efforts made during his previous life in Megalopolis. But when he applied himself to history, philosophy, and the writing of works of religious instruction he was probably entering new fields of endeavour and giving experimental proof of that increase in his range of ability that, according to theory, any man can expect to enjoy in his next life who throughout this life has never ceased trying to learn. "He seems to me a very foolish man," wrote King Alfred, "and very wretched, who will not increase his understanding while he is in the world, and ever wish and long to reach that endless life where all shall be made clear."

Historians may differ regarding the relative importance that should be attached to different aspects of Alfred the Great's vast range of accomplishments, but the one day in his life which appears to have a significance from our point of view deeper than any other, is the day which is of least importance historically. It is the day he burned the cakes.

Plutarch records that on a certain occasion when he was General of the Achaeans, Philopoemen was invited to be the guest at dinner of a certain personage he knew in Megara. He arrived early, before his host, and such was the plainness of his features and the simplicity of his dress that the lady of the house took him for one of his own servants who had been sent in advance to help her with the preparatons. So she took him into the kitchen, and told him to take off his coat and start chopping wood - a task which he obediently performed until his host arrived and found him at it. "What is the meaning of this, Philopoemen?" asked the host. "I am paying the penalty," answered the General in broad dialect, "for my ugly face."

King Alfred's appearance must have been equally plain to have deceived the woman on the door of whose cottage he knocked after he had been defeated by the Danes in Somerset. When she took him for a yokel and told him to mind the cakes while she was out, did there not surge up into his conscious mind a resounding echo from his unconscious memory, giving him a powerful sense of *déja vu*, that uncanny feeling that *this has all happened before*? We can picture him sitting there alone in the cottage, sunk deep in thought, racking his memory for a clue that would call to mind how, when, and where, that same scene had been pre-enacted. And as he sat there lost in reverie he forgot all about the cakes and did not notice the smell of burning coming from the oven. It was typical of the man that when the woman returned and scolded him for his incompetence, he took her scolding in good part as the penalty for his plainness.

Chapter Seven
THE LIBERATORS

The Gracchi = Simon Bolivar

In the second half of the second century B.C. the class struggle by which the history of Rome had been chequered right from the city's foundation, entered a new and uglier phase. Two brothers, TIBERIUS GRACCHUS (B.C. 163-133) and GAIUS GRACCHUS (B.C. 153-121) came forward as champions of the politically and economically underprivileged against the entrenched power of the aristocracy; and both lost their lives in the struggle.

The Gracchi were themselves aristocrats. If they had been ambitious for power they could have obtained it easily enough through normal constitutional means. The high road to the consulship was open to them. But, indoctrinated from boyhood by their high-principled mother with the lofty Roman ideals of service and sacrifice, they were moved by compassion for the underdog, and their sense of justice was outraged by the spectacle of fat inherited estates growing effortlessly fatter on the ill-rewarded toil of the inarticulate masses.

First Tiberius and then Gaius fought to liberate the people from their economic bondage and to redress the inequalities of wealth and privilege. They strove also to give equality of legal status and political opportunity to Rome's former Italian subjects, now her allies, by admitting them to Roman citizenship. But while they fought for justice they were opposed by law, for the law was then, as always, on the side of the constitutional status quo. The Gracchi found it impossible to secure their reforms by constitutional means, and each in turn fell foul of the law rather than give up the attempt. But

79

they had too much inbred respect for the law to be willing to defy it wholeheartedly. They shrank from arming themselves with the illegal force that alone could have brought their cause to victory, whilst nevertheless breaking the law in matters of constitutional detail. By so doing they gave an excuse to their opponents to resort to unlawful means against them. Each in turn, Tiberius in B.C. 133 at the age of thirty, and Gaius at the age of thirty-two seeking to avenge his brother's death twelve years later, was accused of seeking supreme power for himself, declared a public enemy, and murdered.

According to our theory, a man who puts the greatest effort of which he is capable into a creative enterprise and is frustrated by forces that he is not strong enough to overcome will be born again in a later life with increased power to battle with such forces. If, in this case, the two brothers' similar characters and aspirations caused their souls to come together during death and to merge into one, then we should expect to find in a later civilization the world of entrenched privilege and power shaken to its foundations by a revolutionary reformer of truly titanic strength. Such a man appeared in the western hemisphere in the person of the Spaniard SIMON BOLIVAR (1783-1830), soldier, statesman, political philosopher, and orator, who liberated from the oppressive rule of the antique Spanish monarchy the peoples of Venezuela, Colombia, Panama, Peru and Bolivia.

Like the Gracchi, Bolivar was born of a wealthy aristocratic family, and the dominating influence of his boyhood was his mother. From early youth he was inspired by the same ideals of service and sacrifice. His political aims, too, were essentially the same as those of his Roman progenitors: justice in the distribution of wealth and a proper share for all in political power. But he had learned one important lesson from his Roman experience: that these aims could not be realised by constitutional means, and therefore his only hope of success lay in resorting to force. Bolivar therefore devoted his whole life and energies to the task of liberating the Spanish colonies from Spanish rule as the first prerequisite of the establishment of economic and political justice in South America. Appropriately, it was when he was in Rome at the age of twenty-one that Bolivar, standing on the Monte Sacro where the Roman plebs had first seceded from their patrician rulers in B.C. 494, swore an oath to free his people from their colonial yoke.

As we would expect from his spiritual ancestry, Bolivar's generalship was not of a high order, for the Gracchi had little military experience. His success was due to the burning zeal with which he inspired the subject peoples, a zeal that was solidly grounded on a profound knowledge of history and of political philosophy. In his penetrating analyses of the evils of the Spanish colonial system, in his far-sighted prescriptions for reforms, and in the realism he applied to the drafting of constitutions adapted to the backward state of the people he was liberating, Bolivar's mind reveals the qualities of the great Roman statesmen that he had surely been in his former incarnation.

Like the Gracchi, Bolivar was accused by his enemies of seeking supreme power for himself. On more than one occasion he was compelled to take it and become a dictator, but the wielding of power was against his natural inclination, and on each occasion he laid it down of his own accord.

Despite the success of his liberation movement, Bolivar died a disappointed and disillusioned man. The people to whom he had given outward, or political, freedom did not deserve the gift, for they were not yet inwardly free: they lacked knowledge and self-control. Unable to restrain themselves, they fell to quarrelling and fighting. "He who serves a revolution ploughs the sea" was Bolivar's dejected comment on his life's work. Had the Gracchi been successful in their endeavours, doubtless they too would have reached the same conclusion.

Chapter Eight
FATHER AND SON

While Simon Bolivar was performing miracles of endurance in the accomplishment of his herculean task in the far West, another liberation movement, but of a very different kind, was taking place in the East. In Egypt, after the withdrawal of the French army following Napoleon's defeat in the battle of the Nile, there followed a period of confusion from which the figures of MOHAMMED ALI (1769-1849) and his son IBRAHIM PASHA (1789-1848) emerge as the founders of a new but short-lived independence.

Born in Albania, then part of the Ottoman Empire, Mohammed Ali spent the first thirty years of his life as a merchant in that country, where his son also was born. He rose to power in Egypt through his command of an Albanian regiment in the service of the Turkish Sultan. It was a time of trouble: the Sultan's hold on his Egyptian territories was weak; there was conflict between the Pasha (the official governor of Egypt) and the former rulers of the country, the Mamelukes, who were supported by the British; and a mutiny took place when there was not enough money to pay the Pasha's Albanian troops. After much blood had been shed in civil strife, Mohammed Ali, who had shown strength and determination in dealing with the mutineers, was elected Pasha by the council in Cairo (1805) and some time later his appointment was reluctantly confirmed by the Sultan.

With a mixture of ruthless efficiency and treacherous cunning the new governor established his authority impregnably by the extermination of his enemies, including a force of 5000 British soldiers who were landed at Alexandria in 1807. Hundreds of British heads were taken to Cairo and stuck on posts to line an avenue.*

The following year Mohammed Ali set about creating a modern army in the western style and building a fleet, using French officers and engineers for the purpose. To meet the cost he confiscated all freehold land in Egypt, making the owners his tenants, and turned the supply of many essential commodities into Government monopolies. To the command of his new army he appointed his son Ibrahim, who in due course was to prove himself a general of outstanding energy and determination and a tactical genius comparable with the greatest generals of world history. For the next forty years father and son together pursued a policy of aggrandisement that changed the balance of power in the Mediterranean, ranked Egypt amongst the foremost powers of the region, and came within an ace of overthrowing the Ottoman Empire itself.

After he had successfully suppressed the remnants of the Mamelukes who had fled to Nubia, Ibrahim was sent to Arabia to complete the conquest of the fanatical Wahhabi tribesmen whom his father had already expelled from their violent occupation of the holy cities of Mecca and Medina. The

---

* This barbaric act was avenged 75 years later. Egypt was then in a state of bankruptcy caused by the extravagances of the Khedive Ismail, and she had defaulted on her foreign debts. Anglo-French efforts to restore financial order by advice and persuasion failed. In 1882 a revolt took place against Turkish misrule, and after a massacre by an Arab mob the British government decided to intervene. Troops were landed at Ismailia and suppressed the revolt at the battle of Tell-el-Kebir. A British garrison was to remain in occupation of the country for the next 50 years. In 1907, after 25 years of effective British administration and 100 years after the disaster in Alexandria, the agent and consul-general, Lord Cromer, was able to report on his retirement that Egypt was then in a state of unprecedented prosperity.

operation was extremely arduous and dangerous, involving the crossing of 400 miles of desert; but after two years of energetic campaigning during which Ibrahim endured all the privations and hardships of his men, the Wahhabi stronghold was reduced and their forces destroyed.

In 1825 Ibrahim was sent with an army to Greece to help the hard-pressed Turkish forces in the Greek War of Independence. His arrival turned the tide of war decisively in favour of the Turks, and only the intervention of three Great Powers, - Britain, France, and Russia, - who destroyed the Turkish fleet at Navarino (1827) saved the Greeks from destruction and forced Ibrahim to withdraw.

Mohammed Ali was now strong enough to deal on equal terms with the Sultan himself. He demanded to be made permanent and hereditary Pasha of Egypt and to have added to his dominion the pashaliks of Syria and Damascus. When the Sultan demurred, Mohammed Ali threatened to declare Egypt an independent power, and Ibrahim was sent with an army to take Syria by force. In a hurricane campaign of little more than a year's duration (1832-3), Ibrahim reduced the fortress of St. Jean d'Acre, seized Gaza, Jerusalem, Jaffa, Damascus, Aleppo and Homs, defeated two Turkish armies in pitched battles, reached Adana, and crossed the mountains into the heart of Anatolia. Here, at Konia, in a crowning victory over the Grand Vizier, Reshid Pasha, who came to meet him fresh from a victorious campaign against an insurrection in the Balkans, Ibrahim crushed the last of the Turkish forces which the Sultan was able to throw in his path. Constantinople was now at his mercy. He had but to advance, and the capital would have been his.

But Ibrahim advanced no further. What stopped him was, once again, the intervention of the Great Powers. A Russian fleet appeared in the Bosphorus and the Sultan was persuaded to buy off Mohammed Ali by giving him what he wanted. Ibrahim was recalled to Syria, where he was presently installed as the lawful Pasha. This was the high point of his career.

Seven years later, in 1840, the quarrel between Mohammed Ali and the Sultan broke out again. This time the Powers supported the Sultan and occupied Beirut. The Syrian populace rose against the extortionate tyranny that Ibrahim had imposed on them and, his sea communications cut, he was forced to evacuate the country.

Ibrahim spent the rest of his life in peace. In 1846 he paid a visit to western Europe, where it was observed that he was extremely fat. When Mohammed Ali's mind gave way in senile decay, (possibly syphilis) Ibrahim became regent; but his death occurred the same year (1848), shortly followed by that of his father.

* * * * *

Looking back to Roman History one is struck by the extraordinary similarity of the lives of these two great Egyptians with those of two great citizens of a state a little further west on the same shore of the Mediterranean sea. HAMILCAR BARCA (270-228 B.C.) and his son HANNIBAL (249-183 B.C.) fought for Carthage against Rome as Mohammed Ali and Ibrahim fought for Egypt against Turkey in the same spirit of ruthless determination and with the same sudden initial success and ultimate failure. But the two Carthaginians loom larger in ancient history than their Egyptian counterparts do in modern history, because the former were locked in a life and death struggle with the rising power of a city that was destined to rule the world, while the latter were engaged in a domestic conflict with a power already on the verge of collapse. In absolute terms their respective achievements in the political and military spheres are strictly comparable.

Hamilcar Barca rose to power in Carthage through his victorious command of a mercenary force in Sicily which mutinied on its return to Carthage when not enough money was made available to pay the men. Hamilcar showed strength and determination in the way he handled the mutiny, and, in the general confusion of which it was a symptom, he was given the supreme power in the state. He quickly restored order at home by eliminating his enemies and then set to work to organise, train, and equip a modern Carthaginian army. This done, he led an expedition to Spain where he established a dominion which was to serve as the base for an assault on Rome, the hated rival of Carthage to the north and already victor in the First Carthaginian War.

There the paralled with the life of Mohammed Ali stops short, for Hamilcar was killed in battle in Spain while still in his early forties.

Hannibal succeeded both to his father's power and to his ambitions. He completed the conquest of Spain, and then by an extraordinary feet of endurance in the face of apparently insuperable difficulties he led his army, including a large number of elephants, over the Alps into Italy in winter. Only half the army survived the ordeal; Hannibal himself shared all the hardships with his men.

In two years Hannibal marched the length and breadth of Italy, took city after city, defeated three Roman armies, and finally at Cannae in 216 B.C., utterly destroyed the last forces that the Romans were able to put into the field against him.

The city of Rome was now at Hannibal's mercy. But he advanced no further. Instead, he turned south. The opportunity to take the city never recurred. This was the high point of his career.*

The war now reached a stalemate, and Hannibal spent the next thirteen years in South Italy, maintaining his army with increasing difficulty in the face both of growing hostility from the inhabitants and persistent Roman efforts to regain their lost allies. In B.C. 203 he was at last recalled to Carthage to defend his capital against a Roman army under SCIPIO AFRICANUS (B.C. 236-183) (in whom we may perhaps recognise the DUKE OF WELLINGTON (1769-1852). In the following year the great Carthaginian general met his Waterloo at the battle of Zama. Driven from Africa, he took refuge with various Asian kings at whose courts the Romans persistently hunted him, until he was finally driven to take poison within a few miles of the place that later became the city of Constantinople.

* Historians both ancient and modern have been puzzled by Hannibal's failure, so uncharacteristic of him, to follow up his victory at Cannae by an assault on the defenceless capital. This is one of the classic mysteries of ancient history. One possibility, suggested by the parallel of Ibrahim's failure to follow through to Constantinople after the battle of Konia, is that Hannibal was called off by his government at home acting under pressure from a Great Power.

Egypt, under Ptolemy IV, had a strong interest in maintaining a balance of power between Rome and Carthage. At the battle of Raphia in 217 B.C., the year before Cannae, Ptolemy had decisively defeated an attack by Syria on his eastern frontier. It would not be surprising if, alarmed by Hannibal's victories in Italy, he had then feared for the security of his more vulnerable western frontier and had ordered his fleet into the Gulf of Tunis to appear off Carthage as a warning to the Carthaginian government that, if Rome fell, Egypt might take pre-emptive action against their then practically undefended city. This would explain why Hannibal decided to move south into Apulia, whence he would be able to take ship to Africa at short notice should the need arise.

The coincidences thus noted in the lives of the two Carthaginians and those of their Egyptian successors may be besummarised as follows:

Hamilcar	Mohammed Ali
- rose to power in Carthage for success in quelling a mutiny.	- elected Pasha of Egypt for success in quelling a mutiny.
- eliminated enemies at home, then set about creating a modern army.	- eliminated enemies at home then set about creating a modern army and building a fleet.
- annexed territory in Spain by conquest of local tribes, in preparation for war against Rome.	- annexed territory in Arabia by conquest of local tribes, in preparation for operations against the Porte.
- killed in action in Spain leaving his son Hannibal to carry on his work.	- continued to fight for Egyptian independence, working through the agency of his son Ibrahim.

Hannibal	Ibrahim
- born when his father was 20 or 21.	- born when his father was 20.
- led his army across the Alps in winter, sharing severe hardships with his troops.	- led an army across 400 miles of Arabian desert, sharing severe hardships with his troops.
- in two years' campaigning in Italy, won a series of battles against Roman armies, culminating in a crushing victory at Cannae.	- in less than two years, advanced through Palestine and Syria into the heart of Turkey, winning a series of battles which culminated in a crushing victory at Konia.
- did not follow up his victory by marching on the undefended city of Rome.	- did not follow up his victory by marching on the undefended city of Constantinople.
- after being finally defeated at Zama, travelled from one eastern country to another hunted by the Romans, and died by his own hand in Asia Minor.	- spent his last days in peace, some time as Governor of Syria, some time travelling in western Europe, and finally as regent of Egypt when his father became imbecile.

The improbability of these coincidences being purely fortuitous must be assessed in the light of the fact that the two Carthaginians were the two most brilliant stars that shone in the firmament of military might on the southern side of the Mediterranean during Classical antiquity, and the two Egyptians were likewise the two most brilliant stars that shone there in modern times.

Chapter Nine
ROMAN STATESMEN OF THE
MODERN AGE

The similarity of thought and outlook between the turbulent period that marked the end of the Roman Republic and our own troubled times has often been remarked. It is one reason why the study of Roman history by classical students in modern schools centres round that period which may be called, after its greatest character Julius Caesar, the Julian Age. Thanks to the writers of the Augustan Age which followed, the personalities of the great men and women of the Julian Age stand out across the gulf of two thousand years in sharper focus and with greater clarity of detail than that with which we can discern the characters of people of equal stature who lived in the intervening period. And because of the similarities it is fitting to classify those two periods at the end of the Roman Republic and the beginning of the Empire along with the nineteenth and twentieth centuries of the Christian era in the West and describe them together as the *Modern Age*.

One day it will doubtless be possible, after detailed research into classical and modern literature, to fill many chapters with detailed descriptions of the lives of distinguished personalities who can be identified with reasonably high degrees of probability as passing through the world in this Age in successive incarnations. In this chapter it is sufficient to identify only a handful of such characters and to portray them in brief outline, in order to deduce therefrom the current trend in the duration of orbital periods. At the same time we shall take this opportunity to use this historical evidence to point up some interesting facets of the working of the reincarnation process.

First, JULIUS CAESAR himself (102-44 B.C.); warrior, statesman, orator, and historian.

As a soldier, Caesar was not a great strategist or careful master-planner of campaigns. He was something of an opportunist, believing in the invincibility of his own star, and more than once wresting victory from disaster by a combination of personal courage, audacity, and sheer good luck. The gods seemed always to be on his side - a fact which was not lost on the superstitious minds of his contemporaries and was one reason why they were led so easily to believe that after his death he had been taken up into heaven to join his divine protectors.

Likewise in his capacity as a statesman, Julius was no long-term planner; nor had he the gift of organisation or of choosing the best men for the job. In short, he was an indifferent administrator. No one knows what he would have done with the Roman constitution if he had lived, and the probability is that he did not know himself. If he had had a clear plan for the reorganisation of the republic, it may be doubted whether he would have prepared to set off in personal command of his expedition to Parthia in that fateful month of March, B.C. 44. It seemed that he almost welcomed that opportunity to absent himself from Rome as a way out of the impasse into which his domestic policies had led him.

The qualities which made Julius Caesar one of the greatest figures in world history were rather more personal ones. He was through and through a Roman. All the qualities which made the Romans great stood out in high relief in the character of Caesar: his indomitable courage and bulldog tenacity of purpose, his refusal ever to accept defeat, his sincerity and absolute integrity, his magnanimity - though he could be cruel and heartless on occasion, - his somewhat ponderous sense of humour, his liberality and sympathy with the feelings of the common man. These, together with his outstanding achievements in the field and his unshakable belief in the greatness of his own and his country's destiny, endeared him to his friends, while his ambition to rule and his overbearing will made him feared and hated by his enemies.

Only one man in modern history stands comparison with Julius Caesar. In WINSTON CHURCHILL (1874-1965) the spirit of Britain was epitomized as was the spirit of Rome in Caesar. His qualities as warrior, statesman, orator, and historian were the same as Caesar's, but moulded and developed by effort and experience.

As a military leader Churchill's capability was little, if at all, better than Caesar's because of the uninterrupted success of his military career in Roman history. As a statesman, however, he was taught a sharp lesson. From the daggers of Brutus and his fellow conspirators he learned to be tolerant of opposition and scrupulously observant of parliamentary tradition. In his capacities as orator and historian, Caesar so developed his simple direct style that it blossomed in Churchill into some of the greatest masterpieces of English prose.

Caesar's efforts to develop his talents to the utmost were rewarded not only by the heightening of those talents to the pitch of perfection but by the capacity to acquire new talents. Churchill's abundant vitality could not be contained by his political and literary activities but overflowed into the realm of art. And as he himself once jokingly remarked that he hoped to spend a large part of the first few thousand years of his after-life in painting, we may expect to see him again, when the time comes for his return to earth, gaining fame more by his merits as an artist than in the field of politics.

Churchill's physical appearance does not closely resemble Caesar's. The latter's face was lean, his cheeks hollow, and his body spare. Churchill's chubby features were the reverse.

JULIUS CAESAR
(102-44 B.C.)

WINSTON CHURCHILL
(1874-1965)

The reason for the difference is this. Caesar spent most of his active life on horseback and in strenuous physical exertions. In his next life, therefore, his body's metabolism was developed to cope with similar trials. But Churchill's activities were mostly performed seated in a chair, so the physical energy his body had prepared for muscular exertion was not needed and was stored as fat.

One other physical feature may be noted. Caesar had a remarkably long neck. But he was a vain man, highly sensitive with regard to his personal appearance, and it is not unlikely that as a lad he suffered from the jibes of his fellows about the length of his neck. His offended vanity would cause this defect to be over-corrected in his next life, and so Churchill was born with a neck so short as to be almost non-existent.

Great historian though he was, Churchill had one big blind-spot in his knowledge of history. He had never studied the Classics. The history that he knew was the history of our present European civilization, and especially the history of England since 1066. This was a period of continuous 'compression'. The engineer who confines his study of the working of an internal combusion engine to what happens during the compression stroke in one cylinder is not likely to have much idea of what will happen after the piston has reached the end of its travel. So Churchill was without inspiration when it came to the settlement of post-war Europe and took little interest in the problems of reconstruction.

The reason for Churchill's almost rude disregard of the Greeks and Romans was, it seems, a kind of suppressed jealousy. When he first entered Parliament it was still fashionable for Members to quote Latin tags in their speeches - and for anyone who knows enough Latin there is an appropriate tag for almost every situation. Churchill wanted to be the first to utter those pithy apophthegms that reverberate across the centuries, and he felt that the Romans had secured an unfair advantage in being before him in the field. Little did he suspect that he himself had once been the greatest Roman of them all!

So great a man as Julius Caesar could scarcely pass through the world again without leaving unmistakable traces of his passage, even on his half-orbital conjunction. He died in Rome at the spiritual heart of the western world, so we look for him to be born again on the central axis, which was then moving north westwards across France to England. There, a thousand years later in Normandy, appeared the giant figure of WILLIAM THE CONQUEROR (1027-1087), a warrior and statesman comparable in stature with Caesar and Churchill, and a man of similar character.

Among the many motives which led William to launch his successful invasion of England in 1066 may there perhaps be traced a subconscious memory of an uncompleted attempt to subjugate that troublesome island in B.C. 55 and 54? If so, he left no doubt this time that the job was well and truly done. But neither Romans nor Normans had any right to invade Britain. It was only just, therefore, that in his next life when the same warrior-statesman was born on the north side of the English Channel, he should launch across it the world's mightiest invasion in the opposite direction.

When Julius Caesar was murdered, the man who expected to succeed him was his able but unreliable general MARK ANTONY (B.C. 83-30). A man of violent contrasts, Antony was endowed with an immensely powerful physique. Hercules, a reputed ancestor, was his boasted model. His bodily strength was matched by the strength of his physical desires which not infrequently got the better of his rational mind. His life oscillated between periods of prodigious exertion, when he would expose himself to extreme dangers and the most severe hardships, and times when he would wallow in the extremity of luxury and drunken debaucheries. Mars, Bacchus, and Venus all held him fast by turns.

Mark Antony had the courage, audacity, and tactical skill to be a great general, but he lacked the patience; and, though a gifted orator in a bombastic emotional style, he was too blunt to be a good parliamentarian. His vaunted sexuality, philistine tastes, and coarse behaviour gained him the affection of his troops but antagonised the aristocracy and made it impossible that he should ever become the leader of a united nation.

The cause of Antony's undoing was his fondness for women generally, and for one woman in particular. The woman who had conquered Julius Caesar and held him, though not for long, captive in Egypt found Antony an easy prey. From the time when Queen Cleopatra, in answer to an imperious summons from the victor of Philippi, went to Cilicia, overwhelmed him with her oriental splendour, and compelled him to come to meet her on her barge, hers was the dominating influence in his life. Under that influence he arrayed himself in Egyptian attire, assumed the pomp and majesty of royalty, and would have proclaimed himself monarch of the East. Had Antony been victorious at Actium (B.C. 31) there would have been no Roman Empire; Rome would have become the local capital of a western province in an empire modelled on that of Alexander the Great and centred on the city which that conqueror had founded on the eastern mouth of the Nile.

In the last miserable months that he spent with Cleopatra after their defeat, waiting for young Caesar Octavian to come and take them, Antony had time to reflect on the follies that had ruined him. It was too late to repair his shattered fortunes in this life, but not too late to profit by his experience when he returned to live again.

MUSTAFA KEMAL ATATURK (1881-1938) the founder of modern Turkey, had much the same personal characteristics as Mark Antony but a very different fortune. A first-rate general and a rousing speaker, he showed an instinctive understanding of western European methods of thought and conduct and devoted himself to the task of emancipating the Turkish people - especially the women - from the medieval oriental customs by which they were still fettered, and to converting Turkey into a progressive western style republic.

Ataturk's success in this tremendous enterprise was due to the herculean energy with which he drove himself and his people forward. Although he interspersed his prodigious exertions with periods of wild dissipation, he did not this time fall victim to the captivating influence of a scheming woman. When he died (of cirrhosis of the liver) it was not shamefully by suicide after an inglorious defeat, but loved and honoured as a mighty hero and the saviour of his country.

The Roman statesman whom Julius Caesar as a young man admired the most was his uncle by marriage, Caius MARIUS (155-86 B.C.), a man of plebeian descent whose ambition for power was stronger even than Caesar's. A great general, he championed the cause of the common people against the right-wing conservative elements led by SULLA (138-78 B.C.). A bloody conflict was fought between the two leaders, each of whom became dictator and public enemy by turns. Neither of them had enough respect for the law to allow constitutional forms to stand in the way of their personal ambitions. Both men when in power set about the extermination of their political opponents by ruthless means that amounted to a reign of terror.

In modern democracies the place that in Roman times was held by the sword is held by the pen. Political objectives today can be achieved and opposition crushed not by the captaincy of private armies but by the ownership of private newspapers.

MARIUS   LORD BEAVERBROOK
(155 - 86 B.C.)   (1879 - 1964)

The reign of terror that was conducted by Marius put men in fear of losing their lives. The corresponding power today is exercised by the Press which puts many a man in fear of losing his honour or of becoming an object of public scandal - a fear that may well be stronger than the fear of death.

It would not therefore be out of keeping with the progress of the world if Marius in his next life used the Press as his road to power and demonstrated in newspaper campaigns against those whom he conceived to be his country's enemies the skill which he formerly showed in military campaigns against those whom he held to be the enemies of Rome. His identity with Churchill's friend MAXWELL AITKEN, Lord BEAVERBROOK (1879-1964), the Canadian-born proprietor of the most powerful and feared of English newspapers, and dictator of arms production in Churchill's War Cabinet, is suggested not only by these considerations but also by a remarkable facial resemblance.

As for Sulla, our suggestion is that his soul was joined with that of his brilliant general Gnaeus POMPEY (106-48 B.C.), surnamed "the Great", to whom he was bound in life by a strong tie of mutual affection and admiration. Pompey was a great military leader who, in an age of cruelty and fear, was remarkable for his humanity and for the clemency with which he treated his defeated enemies. He was a man of solid virtue and a good administrator but a bad politician. A plain soldier, slow of speech and "uninspired by any spark of erratic genius", he lacked the political sagacity and the personal ambition that were needed to become a great leader of the people. These deficiencies were made good in ample measure by his patron and friend and, if we are right, partner in his next incarnation, Sulla, surnamed Felix, 'the Lucky'.

Although Sulla and Pompey would be described today as right-wing or consevative leaders, and FRANKLIN D. ROOSEVELT (1882-1945) was a left-wing Democratic President of the United States, there was in fact no great difference in outlook between them. All three were practical men, less concerned with ideological principles than with taking whatever practical measures might seem necessary at the time to solve immediate problems. Sulla's legal reforms, Pompey's reorganisation of the corn supply, and Roosevelt's New Deal, all had the same objectives: to restore vitality to an economy that was running down through fear and uncertainty, and to replace a situation of rudderless drift by one of positive control. All three men attached the first importance to meeting the physical needs of the people for whom they were responsible, and none had any great respect for legal traditions. Law was, in their eyes, an instrument of policy, a means of getting things done; and if any laws made long ago as constitutional checks and balances stood in the way of getting things done, then it was time for those laws to be removed.

The circumstances which prevent an American President from taking personal command of an army in he field make it impossible for us to know whether Roosevelt had inherited Pompey's talent as a military commander; but there can be no doubt that he showed a profound knowledge of the art of war in his mobilisation and deployment of the American armed forces and in his direction, as one of the Big Three, of global strategy.

It was reported of Sulla that on his deathbed he told his friends that he faced the other world with equanimity, for his dead wife and son had appeared to him and had bidden him hasten to join them in a life of perfect rest and happiness beyond the grave.

SULLA FELIX
(138 - 78 B.C.)

F.D. ROOSEVELT
(1882 - 1945)

Caesar and Pompey were great men in their day, but Churchill and Roosevelt were greater. We come now to a man whose stature was diminished rather than increased in his next incarnation: their friend and contemporary Marcus Tullius CICERO (106-43 B.C.).

Highly esteemed both in his lifetime and throughout history as the greatest of Roman orators, the master of Latin prose, a distinguished philosopher and man of letters and a politician of considerable influence, Cicero's estimation of his own importance was even higher. A little man with a big head, he was a *novus homo* or self-made man who worked his way to the top by his industry as a lawyer, and who, in spite of his humble birth, succeeded in ranking himself with the aristocracy. He was pompous and conceited and wholly devoid of subtlety. He addressed his friends as he would a public meeting, and the letters he sent them were written more often with a view to publication than as a personal exchange of news and views. He wrote bad verse of which he was inordinately proud.

In the year 63 B.C. Cicero was elected consul and had to deal with a subversive movement in Rome known as the Catilinarian conspiracy. It was a dangerous movement aimed at the usurpation of the government through murder and violence, and it very nearly succeeded. It was thwarted by the vigilance and prompt action of Cicero, who was secretly informed of the conspirators' plans. In a series of masterful speeches he arraigned the ringleader CATILINE (108-62 B.C.) and his fellow bandits with such effect that they were declared public enemies. Catiline then mustered his forces openly and marched on Rome. He had a considerable army, but near Pistoia in Tuscany he was met by a government force under the consul Antonius and in the battle that ensued Catiline was killed. Was it the same power-hungry gangster who in the person of Benito MUSSOLINI (1883-1945) ordered another march on Rome in 1922? If so, we can well understand why on that occasion he himself kept at a safe distance in Milan while the march was in progress. The Italian government's opposition being feeble, that story had a very different ending.

Cicero was not slow to take the credit for Catiline's defeat. This was his proudest moment. For the rest of his life he could never resist the temptation to remind his listeners whenever occasion arose that it was he, Cicero, who had saved the nation from anarchy in the year of his consulship. He even made his consulship the subject of an epic poem entitled *De Consulatu Suo*.

For the rest, Cicero was an ineffective politician but a great constitutional lawyer. As such he was always more concerned to maintain the *status quo* than to improve it, and he was unable to see that the republican constitution under which the little town of Rome had grown to greatness was not suited to enable her citizens to carry out their now world-wide responsibilities. Cicero accordingly set himself against every movement for reform, and opposed the liberal dictatorship of Julius Caesar. Although he had no part in the conspiracy to murder the dictator, he afterwards associated himself wholeheartedly with the conspirators and expressed the wish that they had murdered Mark Antony as well. The latter was his bitter enemy not only on political grounds but because Antony's stepfather had been killed by Cicero as one of the participants in the conspiracy of Catiline. No great injustice was therefore done when Cicero himself was killed in 43 B.C. by Mark Antony, with the consent of Caesar's heir, Octavian.

We search in vain through the history of modern times for a great orator who achieved a fame comparable with that of Cicero. But in DUFF COOPER (1890-1954) we find a man who has all the expected characteristics of the orator's next personality.

A small man with a large head, Duff Cooper was born with a natural talent for public speaking. From his earliest childhood he liked to stand up and recite; as a schoolboy at Eton and an undergraduate at Oxford he shone brilliantly in debates; and throughout his life, whenever he addressed a company he never failed to express himself fluently and elegantly in classical English prose. Born of good middle class parents, he made the most of his unusual Scottish Christian name by linking it inseparably with his common English surname, and succeeded so well in ranking himself amongst the aristocracy that he was able to marry the daughter of a duke.

Duff Cooper showed his taste for poetry and literature at an early age, but he never evinced any interest in law. His choice of a career, first in the diplomatic service and later in politics, suggests that Cicero had become conscious of the barrenness of his legal practice and preferred in his next life to devote himself to the formation rather than the interpretation of laws and treaties. But Duff Cooper's capacity as a statesman was strictly limited. As before, he was conservative, unconstructive, and unable to see the directions in which great changes were called for. In the offices to which he was duly appointed he conducted himself competently, but he left behind no significant accomplishment to mark his passage.

He did not even realise his ambition to become Prime Minister. But he might have done. In his autobiography * he describes how in 1925 he was considered for, and deserved to get, a ministerial appointment in the Foreign Office; but he was passed over in favour of an older man. (Was it because he had a little too much self-assurance to be regarded as likely to make a willing subordinate?). In the event, the chance to shine that should have been his fell instead, a little later, to Antony Eden.

* *Old Men Forget* by Duff Cooper, Rupert Hart-Davis, London, 1953.

In the following year there occurred the critical ten days ot the General Strike when England was threatened with an anarchy not unlike that with which Catiline had threatened Rome. Duff Cooper, still a back-bencher in the House of Commons, sat about in his club with nothing to do. Nobody wanted him. "I have nothing to do" he wrote pathetically in his diary. "Everybody at Buck's is doing something. I only am idle." Such is the penalty for boasting. Truly it is written that he who exalts himself shall be humbled.

In one thing at least, Duff Cooper redeemed an error of Cicero's without having to suffer for it, for Cicero had suffered for it already. After thirty years of marriage, the Roman orator became bored with his good wife Terentia, divorced her, and married a younger woman. Though he tried to justify himself, he was clearly conscience-stricken and must have endured the agony of remorse. His next life's marriage to Lady Diana was a happy union that was dissolved only by his death - a painless natural death at the age of 64. Cicero was one month short of that age when he was murdered.

In the year 60 B.C., in Rome, and again at Lucca four years later, Caesar and Pompey met together with Marcus Licinius CRASSUS (115-53 B.C.) to decide how power in the western world should be divided between them. This was the First Triumvirate: a treaty between the three most powerful men on earth. Caesar was the leader of the Popular party and presently conqueror of Gaul, whilst Pompey was the natural leader of the moneyed classes and conqueror of Asia. How Crassus came to be included is more difficult to understand. He was a multi-millionaire, the richest man in Rome, but money by itself was not the reason for his inclusion. It was because he used his money as a source of power.

Crassus' early years were years of desperate adventure when he was hunted by, and continually escaping from, the assassins of the blood-thirsty Marius who had already slain his father and elder brother. He hid for months in a cave in Spain and then took to the sea as a freebooter. When Sulla marched against Marius, Crassus joined him at the head of a band of outlaws. In Italy he raised a considerable body of troops which he commanded with skill, and actually saved the day for Sulla in a critical battle.* But Sulla did not trust Crassus as he trusted Pompey, and for good reasons. Crassus was not a loyal supporter of a cause, but a sly fox playing his own game. When he captured treasure, he did not hand it over to his commander-in-chief but kept it for himself. At least one man, it was said, Crassus proscribed in Sulla's name solely in order that he might seize his fortune.

When the Roman economy was almost at a standstill after the civil war between Marius and Sulla, and the property market was glutted with the estates of men who had fallen victim to the proscriptions, Crassus invested every penny he could lay hands on in depreciated property to sell again in more prosperous times ahead. He then invented other and more ingenious ways of making money. He bought slaves cheap, trained them in various skills, and sold them at high prices; and he organised a private fire brigade. When a fire broke out Crassus' man turned up and offered the distracted house owner the alternative of selling his house cheap and having the fire extinguished or of keeping the ownership and watching it blaze. By these and other such means Crassus was soon worth many millions.

The wealth he thus amassed was not used to enable him to live in luxury and ease. On the contrary. Crassus worked assiduously all his life. His success was due to unremitting

---

* The battle of the Colline Gate, 82 B.C., in which Sulla defeated a force of 40,000 Samnites who were marching on Rome.

toil and methodical attention to the innumerable details of his complicated transactions. His aim was to get the government and people of Rome into his power, and this aim he largely realised. He had an extraordinary memory for names and faces, and in his calculating brain was stored detailed knowledge of the individual characters, foibles, and secret vices of all the important and many unimportant citizens of Rome. Over large numbers of men in high positions he acquired power by gifts or loans of money, including even Julius Caesar whose youthful extravagances were largely financed by Crassus. Others he controlled through his ability to expose them to scandal. Finally he was suspected of being ultimately responsible, through his agent Clodius, for the organisation of armed gangs of ruffians who, in a city without police, could be turned on easily enough to beat up any citizens of whose conduct he disapproved. Not for nothing was it said of Crassus that "he had straw on his horns" - a reference to the Roman custom of tying wisps of straw to the horns of a dangerous bull.

Such were the means by which Crassus, the master wire-puller, made himself the dictator of the Roman underworld, the most feared and the most powerful man in the city of Rome itself. This was the reason why Caesar and Pompey, who commanded the legions that gave them power in the world outside, invited Crassus to be the third member of the First Triumvirate.

To do him justice, Crassus wielded his power sensibly and, on the whole, for the benefit of his fellow citizens. He was no petty tyrant, subject to the sway of hatreds or jealousies. There was nothing mean about his character, nor did he desire adulation. He was a great patriot who devoted his vast energy to promoting the interests, as he saw them, of Rome. When, therefore, at the second meeting of the Triumvirate at Lucca in 56 B.C., it was proposed that Crassus should undertake a dangerous mission in the East to subdue the Parthians, he did not shrink from the rigours of a tough military campaign. On the contrary, he accepted the challenge and set off, though over sixty, full of high spirits.

But the campaign was short and disastrous. For once the fox was outwitted and trapped by superior trickery. Near Carrhae in north-west Mesopotamia, his army was lured into the desert where the legions, being deficient in cavalry, were at the mercy of the Parthian mounted archers. After a brave defence, Crassus was forced to sue for peace. While in conference with their victors the Roman legates were seized and slaughtered. Crassus' head was presented as a trophy to the Parthian king.

Summing up his life, the historian Sir Charles Oman wrote of Crassus: "he wanted power ... but when he had it he could not use it for he was equally destitute of an ideal and of a programme".*

The same might be said of the third member of the 'Big Three' of modern times, Joseph STALIN (1879-1953). He, too, wanted power but was destitute of an ideal, and his only programme was to apply with remorseless rigour the communist policy of his predecessor, Lenin.

As Crassus died the richest of the rich, so Stalin was born the poorest of the poor. His father was a poor cobbler in the south Russian province of Georgia (not far distant from the place where Crassus died). His mother eked out a miserable living by taking in her neighbours' washing.

As a young man, Stalin was a revolutionary. For years he was hunted by, and kept escaping from, the Tsarist police. He spent many months in prison. In 1903 he attached himself to

---

* C. Oman: *Seven Roman Statesmen* (Arnold, London, 1902, p.202)

Lenin as Crassus had done to Sulla, not because he believed in a cause but because, like many others, he now saw in communism, as Crassus saw in money, the road to power. As profiteering was not appropriate to his role as a communist, Stalin, like Beaverbrook, chose journalism as the instrument of his ambition and by 1917 he was editor of *Pravda*. Five years later his organising ability and his capacity for relentless hard work and methodical attention to detail won him the Secretary-Generalship of the Communist Party, a position in which he found full scope for exercising his extraordinary talent for finding out, remembering, and making use of, the idiosyncratic strengths and weaknesses of his comrades.

When Lenin died in 1924 he left a "testament" in which he recorded his mistrust of Stalin's ambition. He noted how the Secretary-General had "concentrated in his hands an immense power", and he suspected his disloyalty to the cause. But by then it was too late. With consummate dexterity the sly fox insinuated himself into the citadel of power as a member of a triumvirate appointed to succeed Lenin, and then eliminated his rivals one by one.

Having attained supreme power, Stalin used it, as he saw best, for the advancement of his country. He was a great Russian patriot. When war came, Stalin devoted the whole of his vast energies to its conduct, supervising every aspect of the Russian war effort in meticulous detail. His strategy was governed by the subconscious memory of his defeat at Carrhae. Constantly afraid of his infantry being surrounded by German tanks (the modern equivalent of the Parthian cavalry), he withdrew his armies further and further into Russia while devoting the might of Russian industry to the production of tanks. Tanks, tanks, and more tanks, was Stalin's constant demand from his allies; until at last he had enough to strike back and surround a German army. Crassus' defeat at Carrhae was avenged on the Volga.

As a postscript to the lives of Crassus - Stalin I add the suggestion that LENIN (1870-1924), the author of the Russian revolution that brought Stalin to power, was identical with SPARTACUS (died 71 B.C.), the leader of the slave rebellion that terrorised Italy for two years (73-71 B.C.).

Spartacus was a Thracian slave, the victim of an unjust master who forced him and many others to become gladiators although they had committed no crime deserving that sentence. He was a man of considerable intellectual power as well as having great courage, audacity, and powers of leadership. Having escaped from the gladiators' school with a small band of desperadoes, his rebellion gathered strength rapidly from the ranks of oppressed slaves in south Italy and he defeated one Roman army after another sent to destroy him. But his army, by its very nature, was undisciplined and lacked unity of purpose. This was his ruin. Forced by the unruly conduct of his men to engage a powerful Roman army in a pitched battle, he was defeated and killed.

Lenin after his death was deified as one of the two gods of communism, and all his works and sayings were declared sacrosanct and inviolable. The man who was responsible for this deification was Stalin, whose purpose, no doubt, was that he might himself inherit the full extent of Lenin's absolute powers inviolate. This was indeed an act of poetic justice; for the Roman general who, as praetor, commanded the legions by which Spartacus' rebellion was ruthlessly stamped out was Marcus Licinius Crassus.

In the light of this history one may sympathise with Lenin's determination not to be defeated again by insubordination and quarrelling within his party. We may sympathise, too, with his insistence on the need for the "dictatorship of the proletariat", with himself as absolute dictator; and we can understand his instinctive belief in force as the ultimate arbiter of all human destiny. In Spartacus' bitter experiences with his disorderly army of escaped slaves lies the secret of the rigid authoritarian military discipline of thought, word, and deed that characterised communist parties everywhere and made them what they were - slave armies.

Chapter Ten
TWO POETS

The poets VIRGIL (70-19 B.C.) and HORACE (65-8 B.C.), were both alike shy, sensitive men who loved the Italian countryside and who, under the patronage of Augustus and of his great minister, Maecenas, wrote poetry of surpassing beauty. But in their attitudes to life each was the antithesis of the other. One looked forward, convinced of the certainty of a life to come; the other looked backward and was intent on the certainty and permanence of approaching death. Their opposite attitudes are reflected in the contrasting lives and characters of their respective reincarnations as modern poets of the English tongue.

The mind of Horace was the melancholy mind of a pessimist who saw in the changing seasons only the promise of death without resurrection: after spring and summer, autumn and winter. There is only one life and one death, and after death, nothing. In accordance with this philosophy, Horace enjoyed the good things of life while he could - insofar as his gloomy temperament rendered him capable of enjoyment without sadness -, worked no harder than he had to, and kept himself aloof from the "vulgar mob" whose ignorance and brutality he hated as much as he despised their uncultured manners.

Horace's output of poetry was not great, but what he did write was polished to the highest pitch of perfection. He was a fastidious man, gifted with an exquisite delicacy of taste which guided him not only in the composition of poetry but also in his choice of food, wine, and other appurtenances of good living, and in his opinions on morality. He was also master of a biting wit which he directed sometimes at particular men whom he scorned and at other times at popular customs and the ignoble manners of the times. His style was always impeccable and his imagery simple, homely, and direct. He rose to the greatest heights in his lyric poetry. For sheer perfection of match between poetic thought and poetic diction the *Odes* of Horace have never been surpassed in any language.

A. E. HOUSMAN (1859-1936) was a poet less highly esteemed in modern England than Horace was in ancient Rome, but he was endowed with the same poetic capacity as his Latin counterpart. Like Horace, Housman began his life as a clerk in an office. His Maecenas was the University of Cambridge, who appointed him Professor of Latin. The satirical wit to which Horace gave expression in his *Epistles* and *Satires* was vented by Housman in acid comments on his contemporaries from his professorial chair.

Housman's outlook on life was, if anything, even more pessimistic and sombre-hued than that of Horace. His thoughts were never far from the prospect of death. Life, for him, was a "pilgrimage through a vale of tears". The poem which he considered "the most beautiful poem in ancient literature" was the seventh Ode in Horace's fourth book, in which the Latin poet sees the certain advent of death in the coming of winter.

Thaw follows frost, hard on the heel of spring
Treads summer sure to die, for hard on hers
Comes autumn, with his apples scattering;
Then back to wintertide, when nothing stirs.*

For a comparison of Housman's lyric poetry with Horace's we cannot do better than quote Basil Davenport's Introduction

* Horace: *Odes IV*, 7; trans. A. E. Housman, *More Poems V*

to the centennial edition of Housman's collected poems, published in 1959.* "In 1896 his first book of poems, *A Shrophsire Lad*, appeared. It contains sixty-three short poems, all deeply melancholy in mood, all of a chiseled perfection in form, achieving the most exquisite harmonies by the simplest means. In 1922 appeared his *Last Poems*, containing forty-two poems. The total number - of *A Shropshire Lad* and *Last Poems* - which Housman, during his lifetime, selected for publication, a little over a hundred, is almost exactly the same as the Odes of Horace.+ These, too, were deeply melancholy, exquisitely chiseled. There was no progress and no falling off ... Nothing else like this has occurred in the history of literature."

Most of *A Shropshire Lad* was written in a single period of intense mental excitement that Housman experienced in the spring of 1895. This burst of creative activity was also a period of ill health. Most of the poems flashed into his mind complete, or nearly complete, so that he only had to fill in a few gaps by conscious effort. The difference between the conscious and the sub-conscious composition was enormous. Describing how he composed the last poem he said: "Two of the stanzas, I do not say which, came into my head just as they are printed, while I was crossing the corner of Hampstead Heath between the Spaniard's Inn and the footpath to Temple Fortune. A third stanza came with a little coaxing after tea. One more was needed, but it did not come: I had to turn to and compose it myself, and that was a laborious business. I wrote it thirteen times, and it was more than a twelvemonth before I got it right."

* *Complete Poems*: A. E. Housman. Henry Holt and Company, New York.

+ If Horace's *Carmen Saeculare* is included as an Ode, as it should be, and only the forty-one numbered poems of Housman's *Last Poems* are counted, the total number is 104 in both cases.

Now, words no more form themselves automatically into verses in a man's mind than stones on a hillside form themselves automatically into walls. Effort is needed for the creation of verbal as of material order, an effort of selection and arrangement; and insofar as the requisite effort to create the stanzas of *A Shropshire Lad* was not made by Housman's conscious brain it must have been made by his sub-conscious. In fact, it seems that the sub-conscious effort was so great that it absorbed some of the vital energy that was needed for the ordering of his bodily functions and caused him to suffer from ill health. What, then, was the reason for this sudden sub-conscious creative activity, and why did it take place in Housman's brain particularly in 1895?

In that year Housman was thirty-six years old. Horace reached that age in B.C.29, the year in which young Caesar Octavian returned to Rome from his victories in the East to be given a triple triumph, and the gates of the Temple of Janus, which were kept open in time of war, were closed for the first time in living memory. This sudden advent of peace and concord, this bursting out of sunshine after years of storm, was the signal for the release of a flood of literary and artistic enterprise. It is known that most of Horace's *Odes* were composed between 31 and 24 B.C., and it is reasonable to suppose that the peak effort of this creative industry was made in the period 29 to 27 B.C. The latter year is generally regarded as marking the commencement of the Augustan age - the Golden Age of ancient Rome - when Caesar laid down his extraordinary powers and with the unanimous support of Senate and people began his Principate under the title of Augustus. This would suggest that the conscious creative efforts that a person makes in one life may be repeated by his sub-conscious mind in his next life at about the same, or perhaps a somewhat earlier, age. Thus it is to Horace's conscious exertions, inspired by Augustan peace, that we owe the beauty of Housman's poems; and if those poems were short and few, the reason is to be found in Horace's comfortable circumstances on the Sabine estate that Maecenas gave him, where he could live the leisured life of a country gentleman.

Virgil was to Horace as Isaiah to Jeremiah: a prophet of hope to a prophet of gloom. Where Horace's mind was backward-facing and static, disengaged from the forward motion of time like a stationary spinning top which, though spinning perfectly upright, is nevertheless slowly running down, Virgil's mind faced forwards and was intimately geared in with the world's temporal progress whence it derived a dynamic inspiration. To life's challenge Virgil responded not, like Horace, by stepping aside and watching the conflict with philosophic detachment, but by a full personal involvement that evoked from his poetic genius the highest constructive effort of which it was capable. It was an effort not merely to write fine poetry, but to use his poetic gift purposefully as an instrument to help forward the social and economic betterment of the people. From that effort his mind gained increase in breadth and depth, and the strength to conquer fresh fields on his return to life after death.

Virgil's home was a farm near Mantua on the north side of the river Po in the territory then known as Cisalpine Gaul. The Gauls (Celts) had for long been allies of the Romans, their erstwhile conquerors, but until less than twenty years before Virgil's birth they had been treated by them in certain respects as a subject race. In the years 91 to 88 B.C., they took part with others of Rome's allies in a rebellion known as the Social War, the outcome of which was that they were granted full Roman citizenship and equality of franchise. Their political grievances were thus removed, but the ancient Celtic hatred of Rome still smouldered on.

In 41 B.C., when Virgil was twenty-nine, his family was distressed by a special grievance against Rome. His father's farm was confiscated by men acting under the orders of Caesar Octavian who, as triumvir at the age of twenty-two, had been given after the battle of Philippi the difficult and unpleasant task of settling a large number of disbanded legionaries on the land. It was a legitimate grievance. Virgil's father appealed, and the poet himself went to Rome to plead his case. The appeal was heard personally by Caesar, with Maecenas in attendance, and decided in Virgil's favour. The land was promptly restored to his family.

These events made a lasting impression on the young poet's sensitive mind. In place of the ingrained hatred of imagined Roman oppression by which many of his fellow-countrymen were blinded Virgil was imbued all his life with a sense of the wisdom, justice, and beneficence of Roman rule. He became a personal friend of Augustus and Maecenas and under their patronage he attained a prominent position in the literary circle of the capital.

In his youth Virgil showed leanings towards science and philosophy, but these soon gave way to his true inclination towards pure poetry. His first compositions were the *Eclogues*, pastoral idylls which he wrote solely as a means of self-expression. Then, under the influence of Caesar and Maecenas he was persuaded to bend his Muse to purposes of national importance: first, in his *Georgics*, to restoring the fallen status and dignity of Italian agriculture; and later, in the *Aeneid*, to the heroic task of creating a Latin epic of like stature to the epics of Homer, in order to support Augustus' newly founded religion of Rome, the divine city.

Virgil died before he had completed correcting his manuscripts of the *Aeneid*. In his last illness he ordered them to be burned, but they were saved by an order of Augustus. It seemed that he was dissatisfied with the poem and even wished he had never undertaken it. Perhaps there was a feeling at the back of his mind that in glorifying Rome he had in some way betrayed his Gallic countrymen.

It may seem a far cry from the rolling hexameters of the *Aeneid* to the involved symbolism of *The Wanderings of Oisin*, but the thought patterns of the Celtic authors of those two poems are fundamentally the same, the Irishman's being a natural development of the Gaul's, given the different circumstances of his life. The early life of W. B. YEATS (1865-1939) in the green pastures of Sligo, the strong influence of his father on his upbringing, and his early interest in science all echo what we know of Virgil's poetic origins. But the stormy course of the movement for Irish Home Rule and the absence of any strong political personality who could commit Yeats' erratic genius single-mindedly to the task of building an empire subjected his loyalties to far more complex strains than those by which Virgil's mind had been affected, and greatly increased his already great natural difficulty in choosing the mask under which to present himself to the public.

In strong contrast to Housman, who never changed, Yeats never ceased changing, developing, and consciously improving both the style and the subject matter of his poetry. He also consciously developed his personality in other ways by becoming active in social and political movements. He was a great patriot, and when the Irish Free State was eventually established, he was made a Senator; but he remained all his life a close friend and admirer of England.

Yeats's future-directed mind, coupled with his absence of personal ambition, his utter sincerity, and his shy and introspective nature gave him the qualities which are needed to make a prophet. He had indeed, like Virgil, the gift of foreseeing the future, though his visions were dim and blurred. He was a firm believer in reincarnation and in the cyclical motion of spiritual phenomena, and he involved himself deeply in occult beliefs and practices. But he developed also an ideology of his own of which the central idea was what he called the *gyre*, a whirling cone or conical spiral. He visualised both human nature and human history as composed of pairs of interpenetrating gyres, one expanding as the other contracts, like this:

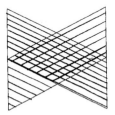

These gyres symbolised objectivity and subjectivity, or the material and the spiritual, or any other trends that rise and fall in cycles. They also have a sexual symbolism; for Yeats, like that other poet-prophet William Blake, whom he greatly revered, was highly sexed, and he saw in the sexual act the union of opposites, the resolution of antinomies, and a symbol of the renewal of the life cycle through reincarnation. For Blake and for Yeats sexual love was not of Satan but of God.

In 40 B.C., when he was thirty years old, Virgil wrote his fourth *Eclogue* in which he prophesied the coming of a new Golden Age and the birth of a child who would "rule with his father's strength a world of peace". Christians later interpreted this poem as prophetic of the coming of the Messiah, like Isaiah's prophecy: "For unto us a child is born, unto us a son is given, and the government shall be upon his shoulder; and his name shall be called ... the Prince of Peace." But the Golden Age that Virgil foresaw was not one that would last for ever; it was the beginning of a new great cycle like that which had begun, according to Roman legend, in the reign of Saturn and had since descended through the ages of Silver and Bronze to the Iron Age.

Magnus ab integro saeclorum nascitur ordo.
"The grand procession of the centuries Begins anew."

In 1896 Yeats, being then thirty-one, wrote that he foresaw that "another Leda would open her knees to the swan" and a new cycle of ages would begin. He felt himself to belong to the new cycle rather than to the one that was ending. Six years earlier he had joined a group called "the Hermetic Society of the Golden Dawn." This was an occult society whose beliefs were based on the ancient Hebrew Kabbalah, with admixtures from Theosophy, Freemasonry, and Rosicrucianism, flavoured by a strong infusion of Christianity. Its members sought through the symbolic practice of magic and alchemy, and through efforts to purify their own lives by spiritual rebirth, to transmute their leaden natures into gold and so prepare themselves for the rebirth of the world. They looked forward to the coming dawn of a new Golden Age; but first there had to be a great war, which would be the world's Armageddon.

In 1919, after the First World War had come and gone and the world seemed as far away as ever from the promised Paradise - indeed, the troubles in Ireland were growing worse - Yeats had a vision of a more sombre kind which he described in his poem *The Second Coming*. He had foreseen the rebirth of Jesus, but the figure of the Christ child was darkened by a shadow:

> "... somewhere in sands of the desert
> A shape with lion body and the head of a man,
> A gaze blank and pitiless as the sun,
> Is moving its slow thighs, while all about it
> Reel shadows of the indignant desert birds ..."

The revelation of a new world order to which this vision pointed was evidently one that comprised not just a renascence of Christianity. Yeats looked for a revival of paganism at the same time, the inauguration of "a subjective pagan era opposite the objective one of Christianity, an annunciation to some new Leda by a swan rather than to some new Mary by a dove."* In an article published in a literary review in 1924 Yeats wrote: "We are Catholics, but of the school of Pope Julius the Second and of the Medician Popes who ordered Michelangelo and Raphael to paint upon the walls of the Vatican, and upon the ceiling of the Sistine Chapel, the doctrine of the Platonic Academy of Florence, the reconciliation of Galilee and Parnassus."**

The Platonic doctrines, like the Christian doctrines that were taught by Jesus (as distinct from some of those now taught in Christian churches), had a hard side as well as a soft, a rough cutting edge as well as a smooth bland surface. It was this rough edge that evidently impressed itself most deeply on Yeats' mind in his vision of the future:

"... but now I know
That twenty centuries of stony sleep
Were vexed to nightmare by a rocking cradle;
And what rough beast, its hour come round at last,
Slouches towards Bethlehem to be born?"

* Rihcard Ellman: *Yeats, the Man and the Masks*; Faber and Faber, p.248. In Yeats' terminology a "subjective" era is one in which the individual personality strives to realise itself to the utmost, as in the Renaissance, while an "objective" era is one in which the individual seeks to escape from his own personality and to submerge himself in the mass, as in Yeats' own time.

** Ibid, p.250

The "rough beast" was clearly the Egyptian Sphinx, "with lion body and head of a man"; but the poet never attempted to explain how that pitiless image came to be associated with the cradle in Bethlehem. He probably did not know that the Sphinx was the personal emblem of that implacable ruler, the friend and idol of his former life, Caesar Augustus.

Chapter Eleven
THE PEACEMAKER

Caesar Augustus is known to history by three different names, corresponding to three distinct periods into which his life was divided. From his birth in 63 B.C. to the murder of his great-uncle Julius Caesar in 44 he was known simply by his family name *Gaius Octavius*. His father was the owner of a country estate in Latium where the boy was brought up by his mother, Atia, with his lovely sister Octavia, to respect the gods and cultivate the traditional Roman virtues. Next, as the posthumously adopted son of the Dictator, he took the name *Gaius Julius Caesar Octavianus*, by which he was known during the troubled period that followed the murder. Finally, in 27 B.C., after his victories had been celebrated in a triple triumph, Octavian, now undisputed master of the Greco-Roman world, laid down his extraordinary powers and was honoured by the Senate's conferring on him the title *Augustus*. That title he enjoyed as *Princeps civitatis*, or First Citizen of Rome, for the forty years of his Principate until his death in A.D. 14.

These three stages in the life of Augustus may be designated respectively periods of (1) character-forming and basic education, (2) vocational training and toughening experience, and (3) service in the creative task assigned to him by Providence. That task was the conversion of the political, social and moral shambles of the latterday Roman republic into a united, peaceable, well-ordered empire governed by an honest and competent administration. (Augustus was not to blame for the fact that the servility of the senate coupled with the excesses of later emperors caused his carefully constructed constitutional Principate to degenerate into an absolute monarchy).

CAESAR AUGUSTUS, (63 B.C. - A.D. 14) wearing the Diadem, as
King of Egypt

I think it likely that the idea of founding an empire first occurred to Octavius when, after the murder of Julius Caesar in circumstances uncannily similar to those that had surrounded the murder of Philip of Macedon in 336 B.C., he felt himself divinely summoned to follow in the footsteps of Philip's son, Alexander the Great. At that time the idea must have seemed to him no less difficult - not to say impossible - and no less dangerous than the idea of leading the Israelites out of Egypt must have seemed to Moses when it was first conceived in his brain. But Octavius recognized that in the vital interests of his people the job he believed he had been called upon to do had to be done by somebody, and that he, and he alone, was equipped with both the natural talents and the political and social standing that were necessary to get it done. He was gifted with a clear logical brain, free of political or religious prejudice, natural tact and sensitivity to other people's feelings, moral courage to resist undue pressures, and a tireless capacity for dogged perseverance in pursuit of his chosen objective. On top of these gifts, and perhaps because of them, he had been named by the great Dictator as sole heir to the conquering name of *Caesar*.

For five hundred years, ever since Tarquin the Proud, the last of the seven kings of Rome, had been driven out, the Romans had nursed an obsessive hatred of monarchy. They had good reason for that hatred. Tarquin had abolished the democratic rights that had been conferred on the people by his predecessor, Servius Tullius, and he had arbitrarily put to death senators and patricians whom he mistrusted. For many years the Romans patiently endured this tyranny until an event occurred that proved the last straw. This was the rape of Lucretia by Tarquin's son Sextus, and her subsequent suicide on account of the dishonour. Outraged by this crime, the people rose up in rebellion and banished the king and his family from the city. The leader of that rebellion was Lucius Brutus, ancestor of Marcus Brutus who, with Cassius, led the conspiracy to murder Julius Caesar in that latest manifestation of the Romans' hatred of monarchy.

All these events would have been recalled by Octavius when he was faced with the decision whether to accept or refuse his inheritance. Fear would have urged him to refuse, as it had done with Moses when he remonstrated with God, saying "Who am I that I should go unto Pharaoh?" But reason told him that if he refused, civil war was bound to follow between Mark Antony and the Republicans, whereas if he accepted there was a fair chance that war could be prevented; and there was no other person in sight who could reconcile the two parties as he could. No other man could give the world the unity and the peace that it so desperately needed. If divine Providence had indeed chosen him for that task, then Providence would ensure that he survived to carry it out.

So Octavius decided, against the advice of his stepfather Philippus, to accept his dangerous inheritance. In the event, the gods duly brought him unscathed through thirteen years of gruelling warfare, in which he experienced defeat as well as victory. This was his period of training for the work ahead. He began it as a frail youth battling with giants bigger and stronger than himself, and ended it as a seasoned warrior and statesman with the same reputation for success, attributed to divine protection, as had been gained by his adoptive father, Julius Caesar.

In the year 36 B.C., at the end of a long and hard fought war against Sextus Pompey and his pirate fleets, Octavian found himself confronted by "that vile blackguard", his fellow triumvir Aemilius Lepidus, with an army of twenty-two legions. This confrontation took place in Sicily, where the islanders still remembered the oppression and extortions of

Lepidus' father when he had been governor of the island a generation earlier. The elder Lepidus has been described as "a man of contemptible character, small ability, and unlimited ambition ... a mere adventurer; there is nothing to show that at any stage of his career his policy was determined by more honourable motives than a resolve to play for his own hand alone."*

The son was no better than the father. Julius Caesar, who was never a good judge of character, had appointed the younger Lepidus "Master of the Horse" and given him command of troops in the city under his dictatorship. In the struggle for power that followed Caesar's death Mark Antony bought the support of Lepidus by promising to procure his election to the office of *Pontifex Maximus*, High Priest of the state religion, which had been held by Caesar. But in the following year when Antony had been defeated by the consular armies and sought refuge with Lepidus' army in Gaul, the latter rudely rejected him. Antony, however, who was as popular with common soldiers as Lepidus was unpopular, entered the other's camp alone and talked the men over to his side, to such effect that they would have killed their own commander had Antony not restrained them.

I mention this episode because it must enhance our opinion of Octavian's courage in attempting against Lepidus in Sicily the same manoeuvre that Antony had successfully used to defeat him in Gaul; for young Caesar must have known that Lepidus would be on his guard against being caught twice in the same way and would surely give orders to have him killed if he entered his camp to address the troops. What actually

---

* Sallust Hist. 1.55, 18 M; Cambridge Ancient History Vol. IX p.314.

happened was described by the military annalist Velleius Paterculus (19 B.C. - A.D. 31) thus:

"The Scipios and the other Roman generals of old never dared or did a braver act than did Caesar (Octavian) at this juncture. Unarmed and dressed in his travelling cloak, protected by nothing but his name, he entered the camp of Lepidus, and, escaping the weapons that were hurled at him by the orders of that vile blackguard, though his cloak was pierced by a spear, he had the courage to carry off the eagle of a legion."

Not one legion only, but the whole of Lepidus' army of twenty-two legions went over to Caesar, and a new civil war was averted.

When Lepidus found himself deserted by his army he was reduced to grovelling at Octavian's feet and begging for mercy. Common justice demanded that he should die, and the victor's normal instinct would have been to slay the villain then and there with his own hand. But Octavian's hand was stayed by a deeper instinct. Lepidus was the high priest of Jupiter, Father of the Roman gods. The gods had just saved him, Octavian, from death; should he now show his gratitude to them by slaying their high priest? Surely not. the deep respect for religion that he had learned at his mother's knee forbade him to commit that sacrilege, so he contented himself with removing the would-be murderer's purple cloak, the official insignia of Lepidus' command as *imperator*. He then let him go free.

I wonder if, when young Caesar reflected on this episode in a later moment of calm, he experienced a sense of *déjà vu*. Did there, perhaps, rise up into his conscious mind a far memory of a day in a former life when, as now, he had narrowly escaped death at the hands of a man whom Providence had then put it in his power to kill? That man, too, was the commander of an army, but he was not a high priest. He was a king - a man who had been anointed king by a high priest in the name of God.

"Then Saul took three thousand chosen men out of all Israel, and went to seek David (to kill him) ... And he came to the sheepcotes where there was a cave; and Saul went in ... and David and his men remained in the sides of the cave. And the men of David said unto him, Behold the day of which the Lord said unto thee, Behold, I will deliver thine enemy into thine hand that thou mayest do to him as it shall seem good unto thee. And David said unto his men, the Lord forbid that I should do this thing unto my master, the Lord's anointed, to stretch forth mine hand against him, seeing he is the anointed of the Lord. So David stayed his servants with these words, and suffered them not to rise against Saul. Then David arose, and cut off the border of Saul's cloak privily. But Saul rose up out of the cave and went on his way."*

David was born in Israel about one thousand years before Gaius Octavius was born in Italy. Like Octavius, his life was divided into three distinct phases. The youngest of the sons of Jesse, a landowner in the district of Bethlehem of Judaea, David's boyhood was spent with his family, where we first hear of him tending the sheep on his father's estate. The religious orientation that was imparted to his natural intelligence by this experience of nature, alone and free on the

* I Samuel 24: 2-7. The order of the verses had been slightly changed to conform with what scholars have regarded as the more likely original version. 'The sides of the cave' refers to chambers and recesses such as abound in some of the labyrinthine caves that are to be found in the hillls west of the Dead Sea.

hillsides for long periods on end, became the outstanding feature of his life. Yahweh, the god of Moses and of freedom, was never far from his thoughts.

The second phase of David's life was a stormy period of war and strife which turned the rustic youth into a seasoned warrior and leader of men. The broad impression that is conveyed by the Biblical narrative of the events of this period is of David's prowess as a fighting man with a strong right arm, rivalling his master, King Saul, and arousing the latter's jealousy by his popularity as a soldier. "Saul hath slain his thousands", sang the women as they acclaimed the army returning from victory over the Philistines, "but David his tens of thousands."

There is no doubt that repeated success in military engagements was the principal source of the tide of popular favour that raised David to the monarchy, as it was to do later in the case of Octavian, but it is safe to conjecture that that success was not due to muscular strength on David's part so much as to intelligent planning. The balance of military might was on the side of his enemies. David's rivalry with Saul, like Octavian's with Mark Antony, was an archetypal episode in the Long War between emergent Intelligence and established Might. Both episodes took place at critical junctures in the history of western civilization. Their message is symbolised in classic style by the story of how the unarmed boy David conquered the heavily-armed giant Goliath not by superior strength but by minimal force applied with ingenuity and skill.

David's association with Saul began when the latter was suffering from melancholia, and the shepherd boy was introduced to him as a skilled harpist who could assuage the King's malady by his music. Established at court as Saul's page and armour-bearer, David formed a close and lasting friendship with the King's son Jonathan. He also stole the heart of his daughter Michal. No doubt it was David's popularity at court, where his youthful charm contrasted strongly with Saul's moroseness, that sowed the seeds of the King's jealousy. This was inflamed by David's military successes, which endeared him to the people. In a fit of jealous rage Saul hurled a spear at David while he was playing the harp. The young man fled for his life.

The later years of this second phase of his career David spent as an outlaw with a band of followers in the mountains of Moab and south Judah. He was there when news reached him of the deaths of Saul and Jonathan in battle with the Philistines.

David was thirty years old when he was called on by the people of Judah to be their king. Scholars have put the date at around 1010 B.C. Like Augustus, he reigned for forty years. After seven years as King of Judah in Hebron, he was elected by common consent of the northern tribes to be their king also, and from then on he ruled over the united kingdom of Judah and Israel. This was the period of his creative work for which his earlier life had fitted him.

As King of Israel and Judah, David's first act was to capture, by a clever stratagem, the seemingly impregnable town of Jerusalem, which at that time was occupied by the Canaanite tribe of Jebusites. There, close to the border between the two territories, he established the government of his united kingdom. In the course of his reign he transformed Jerusalem from a tribal stronghold into a city worthy of its position as the capital of an empire, so that for ever after it was known as the City of David.

In like manner Caesar Augustus so transformed the city of Rome that it was said of him that he found it brick and left it marble.

Although the frontiers of David's empire, like those of Caesar's, were extended and secured by military victories, in neither case was the peace that was won by those victories maintained by military repression. Neither the Israelite nor the early Roman empire was a monolithic structure subject to one man's arbitrary rule. Both founders gave varying degrees of autonomy to subject peoples on the peripheries of their empires; both gave personal attention to the administration of justice within their realms; and both saw in religion a more potent influence than law for the prevention of crime and the maintenance of order.

David believed that he had been sent by God to found a kingdom and a dynasty that would last for ever. "O Lord God", he prayed, "let it please thee to bless the house of thy servant, that it may continue for ever before thee ... and with thy blessing let the house of thy servant be blessed for ever." This may be compared with the more pragmatic prayer that was uttered by Augustus in one of his early edicts: "May I be privileged to build firm and lasting foundations for the government of Rome. May I also achieve the reward to which I aspire: that of being known as the author of the best possible constitution, and of carrying with me, when I die, the hope that these foundations will abide secure."

David's prayer was not granted in his then lifetime. His empire broke up barely fifty years after his death. The foundations laid by Augustus, on the other hand, were still essentially intact five hundred years after the emperor died, and were still recognisable five hundred years later still. The historical record of the Roman Empire is eloquent testimony to the skill as an organiser and administrator of its founder. A modest and unpretentious character having no desire to dominate, bearing the name but lacking the charisma of his adoptive father, young Caesar Octavianus nevertheless took to the art of ruling as a duck takes to swimming. How better can this paradox be explained than by supposing that the instinct that made him from the beginning think and act as the ruler of an empire were inherited from a former life in which he had been just that?

Another indication of an inherited instinct may perhaps be discernible in Octavian's heartless and high-handed attitude towards women, which resembled more that of an oriental monarch than a citizen of republican Rome.

At the age of twenty-three, having divorced his first wife Clodia whom he had married for political reasons, Octavian married his second wife Scribonia and divorced her a year later on the day she gave birth to their daughter Julia. The reason he divorced her was in order to marry Livia, a lady of high birth who was then married to a distinguished senator. Octavian induced Livia's husband to divorce her when she already had one son and was six months pregnant with another.

Augustus remained faithful to Livia for the rest of his life, but towards the end he had cause to regret his early matrimonial involvements. His marriage to Livia was barren, and Julia remained his only child. In 11 B.C., when Julia was twenty-seven and widowed for the second time, he compelled her to marry his stepson Tiberius, who in turn was induced to divorce his wife Vipsania to whom he was devoted. During Tiberius' long absences from Rome Julia used her freedom to indulge in wildly licentious behaviour which became the talk of Rome. By thus disgracing her father's name she avenged the wrong that he had done her mother.

When news of his daughter's adulteries at length reached the ears of the emperor, he banished her to a remote island where she spent the rest of her life with her loving mother, Scribonia, who voluntarily shared her exile.

This and other domestic tragedies, including the deaths of two grandsons and the ineptitude of the third, together with the destruction of a Roman army in Germany, cast dark shadows over Augustus' declining years. Having no surviving issue capable of succeeding to the Principate, he was forced to hand down the empire he had founded to his surly stepson Tiberius.

The declining years of King David were likewise darkened by domestic tragedies; and he, too, faced a problem over the choice of a successor. His problem, however, did not arise from an absence of suitable progeny, but from a surfeit.

In accordance with the customs of the east, David kept a harem of wives and concubines who bore him numerous children. This did not prevent him, however, from becoming enamoured of the wife of a neighbour, Uriah the Hittite, a young officer in the Israelite army. The full story of David's adulterous relationship with Bathsheba, and how he tried in vain to cover it up, is contained in the eleventh chapter of the Second Book of Samuel. He married her after he had procured the death of Uriah by having him placed "in the forefront of the hottest battle." The son she bore him, Solomon, he eventually nominated to succeed him on the throne, but not until after his favourite son Absalom had raised an armed rebellion against him and been killed in the fighting.

Two other characters in this drama can be identified, with a reasonable degree of probability, with later-life incarnations. SAUL was chosen by Samuel to be the first king of Israel on account of his kingly and soldierly physique: tall, handsome, and strong; but in the latter part of his life he developed an increasingly morose, suspicious and jealous disposition. The emperor TIBERIUS was likewise tall, handsome, and strong, a good soldier in his prime, who became a prey to suspicions, jealousy, and fits of melancholia in the latter part of his life. It would seem that the stars of Saul's and David's souls circled round one another in the realm of the departed and returned to earth in the opposite order from that in which they left it.

Certainly, divine justice was done when Saul, who had required David to minister to him as page, armour-bearer, and musician, and later as army commander, and who gave David his daughter in marriage, was born again as Tiberius and made subservient to the will of his step-father Augustus, who made him the commander of his armies and the husband of his daughter.

The other recognisable character is that evil man AEMILIUS LEPIDUS who, thanks to the accident of his being the only man in Rome in command of troops at the time when Julius Caesar was murdered, was appointed in the following year a member of the Second Triumvirate with Mark Antony and Octavian. A self-important, humourless, unprincipled man of overweening ambition and limited ability, it seems that Lepidus saw the Second Triumvirate as a repetition of the First, with the other two members playing the roles of Pompey and Crassus, and himself as Caesar. He made it his aim to dispose of his two colleagues one by one and then, like Caesar, to rule the whole world as Dictator.

This aim was frustrated when first Antony and later Octavian on different occasions, entered the camp of Lepidus alone and talked his men over to their side. Both men spared his life. After the second occasion his military and political career was ended in disgrace, but he was left with the office of *Pontifex Maximus* which he occupied till his death twenty-four years later.

There is no record of Lepidus' activities during that period, but it is reasonable to suppose that, having twice experienced the very real power of oratory at the sharp end, the frustrated politician used the unrivalled opportunities given him by his priestly office to practice to perfection the art of winning over the hearts and minds of large audiences by public speaking. At all events, I suggest that Lepidus' embittered soul with his insatiable lust for power returned to earth in due course as ADOLF HITLER and tried once again - this time by speech as well as action - to realise his ambition to dominate the world.

If this is right, it is instructive to note how the characters of the two protagonists of the Second World War, Churchill and Hitler, were influenced in opposite ways by the opposite treatments they had received in their former incarnations.

Julius Caesar wielded supreme power as Dictator in the Roman Senate, and was murdered on that account by fellow Senators. Next time round, as Churchill, he was scrupulously careful to avoid giving his fellow Parliamentarians any excuse for accusing him of wielding dictatorial power, even in the most perilous crises of the war.

Aemilius Lepidus was spared the death that he had richly deserved by his treacherous conduct in pursuit of a manic ambition to rule the world. As Hitler, he sank to even greater depths of treachery and cruelty in the relentless pursuit of the same objective.

Hitler escaped from human justice when he killed himself in his bunker in Berlin. But there is no possibility that he and his myrmidons will have eluded justice altogether. The inexorable laws of mathematics demand that, sooner or later, and perhaps for ever, they must pay for their appalling crimes by suffering the extremity of pain in accordance with the warnings that were uttered of old, alike by the Greek mathematician and Pythagorean philosopher Plato and by the Jewish prophet, Jesus of Nazareth.

Chapter Twelve
CLEOPATRA

In this chapter I present an unorthodox picture of one of the most fascinating characters of the ancient world, who played a decisive role at a critical juncture of world history. This new insight into the motives of the last Queen of Egypt has become possible now for the first time in consequence of the crumbling in recent years of the previously impregnable wall of prejudice that has been maintained - not without justification - by men all down the ages against any hint of a suggestion that a woman could be their equal, let alone their superior, in the life-and-death struggles of the politico-military arena.

The sources consulted include Appian, Dio Cassius, Cicero, Josephus, Pliny the Younger, Plutarch, and Suetonius.

*　　　　*　　　　*

No list of the great decisive battles of the world is complete without mention of the battle of Actium. Actium marks a watershed, a dividing line between two epochs as sharp as any in history. On one side we look back down the steep craggy ascent of the Roman Republic, boulder-strewn with wars and deeply fissured by party strife. On the other, there spreads the broad smooth plateau of the Roman Empire, the politically featureless but culturally fertile plain of the Pax Romana.

Actium itself was the climax of a long series of fratricidal wars that had split the world asunder and brought western civilization to the very brink of political and economic collapse. By his victory, and the statesmanship with which he followed it up, young Caesar Octavian abolished party politics, welded together the divided eastern and western halves of the Greco-Roman world, and raised the curtain on that happy era named after him, the 'Augustan Age' - the Golden Age of ancient Rome.

The division between the two epochs can be timed precisely. It occurred on September 2nd, BC 31, at about two o'clock in the afternoon. At that moment Cleopatra, Queen of Egypt and self-appointed Commander-in-Chief of the forces of the eastern powers, hoisted a signal on the mast of her flagship in the Gulf of Ambracia, sailed through the middle of her own and the enemy lines out into the open sea, and set course for Alexandria. We do not know exactly what the signal said, but my guess is that it said simply, "Follow Me". At all events she was followed first by the rest of her Egyptian squadron which had been stationed in the rear of the main fleet, and then by Mark Antony, who transferred from his battleship to a fast five-tiered galley, deserted the fight, and sped after his mistress.

The battle was far from having been decided when Cleopatra made that signal. Antony was a great fighter. It is quite possible that if he had stayed to fight it out, the sea victory would have been his. Certainly his land forces were superior to Caesar's, and it is more than likely that if he had led them in a well-planned attack he would have routed the enemy's army. This, in fact, was what he and his generals had wanted to do. But their plan had been vetoed by Cleopatra who insisted on first engaging the enemy by sea. When she and Antony deserted the fight, all their vast forces surrendered, and what had promised to be one of the bloodiest battles ever fought, turned out to be a walk-over. Actium was one of the world's greatest military débâcles.

There are several puzzling features about the battle. The usual view is that Cleopatra took her decision to quit in a moment of panic. According to Dio Cassius, she was unable to bear the tension and anxiety of the battle any longer and lost her nerve -"true to her nature", he added contemptuously, "as a woman and Egyptian". If that were the case, why did she show no signs of distress or remorse when Antony joined her? And if she had not intended Antony to follow her, why did she not send him back to continue the fighting while there was yet time, or at least fly to his arms for mutual comfort, instead of leaving him to sit miserably in the prow of her ship for two whole days with his head in his hands, and refuse even to see him? Cleopatra was, in any case, one of the most courageous women that ever lived, as we shall see. Why had her ship put out to sea laden down with all her golden treasure and a vast quantity of personal belongings, and why were the captains of all her Egyptian ships ordered, to their astonishment, to take their heavy sails on board when the invariable custom was for warships about to engage in battle to leave their sails on shore?

Numerous theories have been put forward by historians in attempts to reconstruct a battle plan for Antony and Cleopatra that accounts for all the facts and makes military sense in the context of the known dispositions of their forces. One German historian wrote a book putting forward a certain theory, and later followed it with another book rejecting that theory and putting forward an entirely different idea. The fact is that no theory yet advanced satisfactorily solves all the problems. Actium remains an enigma. Perhaps the most puzzling question of all is: what was Cleopatra doing there anyway? What motive inspired that most feminine creature to encase her gorgeous figure in armour, reject the most urgent entreaties of Antony and his friends, who for months had implored her to

141

go home, and insist against all precedent on leading her unwarlike Egyptian crews into what everyone expected to be a bloodbath? Why did she not leave the conduct of the war to Antony? She must have known that he was a better general that she would ever be.

To find the answers to these questions we must, I think, probe a little deeper into Cleopatra's character than has been done hitherto. When I say "probe", I do not mean "research", I mean "think".

Dr. Johnson once said, "We must trust the characters we find in history except when they are drawn by those who knew the persons". There is no contemporary record of Cleopatra's character, and the ancient historians who wrote about her did so long after she was dead, and they were mostly either biased or just plain bad. We cannot trust them. We must take their word for the facts of what she did, but let us make our own interpretation of her motives.

Knowing at least some of the events of her early life which reveal the sort of woman she was at heart, let us first put ourselves in her position, try to imagine how she would have felt and thought about the dramatic events that unfolded around her, then see what she did, and make our own deductions as to *why* she did it.

Dramatics events indeed! Drama - that is the keynote of Cleopatra's life. Everything she did and said was dramatic. She herself was above all else an actress, consciously acting a part on the stage of history, taking her turn to enjoy the limelight and reacting to it with a theatrical-sense not surpassed by any other great character in the annals of war and peace.

When Shakespeare wrote *"Age cannot wither her nor custom stale her infinite variety"*, he painted a true picture. But it was not a picture of the true woman. It was a picture of the mask, the infinite variety of masks, which this supreme actress put on in order to fulfil the role that had been assigned to her by Providence. The true woman, as I hope to show, was simple, pure and steadfast in the pursuit of one lifelong aim. That aim was not, as some have maintained, the acquisition of wealth and power for her own pleasure or for her country's aggrandisement; nor was it, as others have contended, the gratification of an inordinate appetite for sex. It was nothing less than the establishment of permanent, universal peace.

That was the aim towards which she strove. Songs of happiness and joy were to fill the air in the grand finale of her life - a royal pageant with the spotlight focused on the Queen of the East, holding hands with the King of the West, inaugurating a reign of eternal peace from which the spectre of war and strife would be banished for ever. That was her dream - a dream which she all but realised. It was only at the very end, when the peace she strove for had already been established, that she realised that the play was, for her, not a musical comedy but a tragedy.

Cleopatra's first entry on to the world stage, like the prologue to an Aeschylean tragedy, set the pattern for the rest of the drama. She enters as no other person has entered, rolled up in a carpet, carried on a man's shoulder, and is laid at the feet of the master of the world, Julius Caesar.

This episode is usually dismissed as an entertaining anecdote, but there is a great deal more to it than that. It is a perfect introduction to Cleopatra's character and to her method of working. It reveals not only her sense of the theatrical, but also her impudent audacity, her originality, her irrepressible sense of fun and her total lack of false dignity or pride. It also shows her as having a deep intuitive understanding of the character of the man she was dealing with, an understanding which, with her other qualities, made her a consummate exponent of the art of psychological warfare. For let there be no mistake about this: Cleopatra was at war, and Julius Caesar was her enemy. *Operation Carpet* was a military operation by which she set out to conquer her enemy - and succeeded.

The circumstances were as follows. In 51 BC. Ptolemy XII, surnamed Auletes, the Flute-player, had died, leaving his kingdom to his daughter Cleopatra, now 18, and her eldest brother Ptolemy XIII, aged 10. In accordance to the custom of the Egyptian pharaohs, brother and sister were married and crowned king and queen.

Before long the high-spirited young queen showed strength of mind by quarrelling with the eunuchs, priests, and generals whose tortuous machinations did service for government in Egypt at the time. A palace revolution took place and Cleopatra found herself banished from her kingdom, leaving the boy Ptolemy as sole sovereign. This was in 48 BC., when Pompey the Great, to whom Cleopatra's father had owed his throne, was defeated at Pharsalus and fled for refuge to Alexandria, hotly pursued by the victorious Caesar with a couple of legions. The boy king's ministers showed their treacherous natures and their lack of understanding of the Roman character by stabbing Pompey in the back as he stepped ashore from a small boat, and greeting Caesar with a present of Pompey's head in a basket. Caesar wept and ordered that the head should be buried in a plot sacred to Nemesis. Before he left Egypt, Nemesis had done her work: all Pompey's slayers had themselves been slain.

The first thing Caesar did was to try to patch up the quarrel between the Alexandrian government and the exiled queen. Cleopatra, with characteristic energy and resource, had raised an army in Syria to fight her way back. Caesar sent a message commanding her to appear before him to plead her cause, so that he might settle the dispute. But she was the rightful Queen of Egypt and she had no desire to plead her cause before any upstart Roman general. In any case, her way was barred by an Egyptian government army that faced on the eastern frontier at Pelusium. She planned to storm her way back by force.

144

Then a better idea struck her. She thought of the carpet, and decided to make love, not war. Embarking in a small boat alone with a powerful Sicilian oarsman named Apollodorus, she was rowed silently into the harbour of Alexandria as it was getting dark. There Apollodorus rolled her up in the carpet - some say it was a kind of mattress - tied the bundle round with string, and carried it on his shoulder into the palace, getting past the guards (who would certainly have killed her if they had known) with the pretext that he was carrying a present for the Roman general from an anonymous donor.

Ushered into the great man's presence, the Sicilian unrolled his bundle and out stepped the most fascinating creature that Caesar ever set eyes on. History does not relate who opened the conversation, but I like to think it went something like this. Turning her back on him without even a glance, she would walk over to a mirror on the other side of the room, adjust her hair and her dress, stretch her arms, and then, cool as a cucumber, walk up to him and, looking at him with childlike innocence, say in her native Greek: *"By Zeus, I had no idea that carpets could be so hard. Tell me, have you ever been rolled up in a carpet?"*

Let us now consider this episode as a military operation, which is exactly what it was because it took the place of a battle. The classic recipe for a successful battle is this. First take your enemy by surprise. Attack him from an unexpected quarter, preferably by night. Before he has recovered from the shock, engage him closely on territory of your own choosing where the forces in which he is strong are of little value and your own can be deployed to maximum advantage. Finally, having won the initiative, never let it go. Keep the enemy dancing to your tune; never dance to his, until you have forced him to surrender.

These textbook instructions Cleopatra followed out to the letter. Having achieved surprise with the carpet, she followed

145

it up after some preliminary skirmishing with a decisive blow. Pretending not to realise that he had, in all probability, been sleeping in her royal bed, and knowing that in any case she could not turn him out by force, she graciously invited him to share it with her. Thus, she turned the tables on the great dictator.

From having been the master in her palace he became her guest, and at the same time she engaged him on territory where his legion would be useless and where, despite his fabled prowess as a lover, she reckoned on being able to easily establish her superiority. After all, she was 21 and he was 54. And she was no virgin. She had already, for political reasons , had an affair with Pompey's son Sextus from whom she had no doubt learned a thing or two about the sexual proclivities of the Roman nobility.

Caesar stayed nine months in Alexandria. For the first six he was occupied by a dangerous war with the Alexandrian people in the course of which the boy king Ptolemy lost his life and Caesar himself came within an ace of losing his. The last three months he spent being royally entertained by Cleopatra, who was now in an advanced state of pregnancy. Together they visited the tomb of Alexander the Great. Then, having showed him all the fabulous sights of Alexander's city, the greatest and most splendid city in the world, she took him in a magnificent floating palace, escorted by four hundred other vessels, on a thousand mile journey up the Nile.

I think it was here - in this idyllic interlude in Caesar's tempestuous life, as he surveyed thirty centuries of history from the Great Pyramid of Cheops to the 400 ft. lighthouse on the island of Pharos, stimulated by the sparkling companionship of the youthful queen of this ancient kingdom - it was here that Caesar began to conjure up a vision of the future governance of the Greco-Roman world. As he talked, his ideas would be eagerly taken in by his companion, and then returned to him again, enlivened and enriched by her sense of drama. Out of this intercourse there was conceived, I think, a Grand Design: the recreation of Alexander's mighty empire on an even mightier scale by the union of East and West under the all-embracing protection of Roman military power. Cleopatra's contribution to this Grand Design would have been to insist, from her instinctive understanding of oriental peoples, that the new Alexander must be invested with all the regalia of kingship.

Caesar would be a king, crowned, sceptred, and enthroned, and like all kings he would be believed to have received his royal power by divine dispensation. She herself, as hereditary queen of the Ptolemaic dynasty, was believed by her subjects to be the incarnation of Isis, and she encouraged that belief by acting the part of the goddess in religious ceremonies. Let Caesar first conquer those realms that were still independent and then put on the royal diadem. The King of the West would then be married to the Queen of the East to rule over a united world, and the union would be sanctified for ever in their seed, of which the first-born was already stirring in the womb.

There was a big Jewish population in Alexandria, and Cleopatra cannot have failed to pick up the current talk of the coming Messiah. In the West, too, there was a growing awareness among discerning souls of a coming world crisis. Soon the poet Virgil would be prophesying in the *Fourth Eclogue* the birth of a child who would free the world from fear and establish a new reign of Saturn, a new Golden Age on Earth. Did the young queen wonder, as many a mother-to-be must have wondered, whether the child that she was to bear might be the wonder-child who was to be the Christ, the anointed King of Kings, sent by Heaven to bring peace on earth and good will to all mankind?

A reverse to Roman arms in Asia called Julius away a fortnight before the birth of his son, Ptolemy Caesar, known as Caesarion. The dictator settled the Asian rebellion in five days and returned to Rome, whither Cleopatra followed him fifteen months later, in October 46, taking her infant son with her. With imperious disregard for respectable Roman opinion, Caesar acknowledged his illegitimate son and installed his royal mistress in a mansion outside the city on the other side of the Tiber. Here she lived for eighteen months, drinking in the heady atmosphere of this vibrant city, entertaining on a tactfully modest scale the leading figures of Roman society, and getting to know intimately the immense strength - and the weakness - of the Roman people.

A whiff of Egyptian incense can, I think, be detected in the episode that occurred on 15th February 44, when Caesar was seated in the Forum and Mark Antony, consul for the year and priest of the festival of Lupercalia, playfully placed a crown upon his head. This was clearly a kite-flying experiment to test the reactions of public opinion. But surely the idea was far too exotic ever to have occurred either to so Roman a Roman as Julius Caesar, or to the unimaginative Mark Antony, without the inspiration of some royal prompter.

Be that as it may, the episode served in the end only to supply one more piece of tinder to heap the explosion which was to shatter the world asunder on the Ides of March.

After she had recovered from the shock of the dictator's murder, what would Cleopatra's attitude be likely to have been in the new situation? Would she have dropped her Grand Design altogether, or would she have continued to hope and scheme for peace in a united world, looking for some worthy successor to take the place of the man she had conquered, and loved, and planned to make king?

Two men disputed the succession. One was Mark Antony, Julius' colleague in the consulship, a hard-drinking, swashbuckling soldier, a man of gargantuan appetites and wildly extravagant tastes, who boasted his ancestry from Hercules (to whose physical stature his own massive frame bore some resemblance), and who carried an outsize sword buckled round a mini-tunic that was designed to show off his Herculean thighs. In his youth he vaunted many feats of amorous virtuosity with actresses and the like, but now, at 40, he was securely under the thumb of his red-haired ambitious virago wife, Fulvia.

The other claimant was Gaius Octavius, a boy of 18 who was still studying at a college in Greece when Julius, his mother's uncle, was murdered. A shy, serious, sensitive, and intelligent young man, Octavius had been brought up in the country with his beautiful and virtuous sister Octavia according to old-fashioned standards of morality, and was endowed with a strong sense of duty. He was a rotten soldier. He loathed fighting and was liable to became physically sick at the mere thought of carnage. History has dubbed him "cold and calculating". These are not opprobrious epithets. They are terms we all of us apply to anyone in a rival position who can see two or three moves further ahead than we can ourselves, who never loses his temper. Such men are infuriating. They are sometimes described as "inhuman", although in fact, if rationality is the feature by which men are distinguished from animals, they have a right on that account to be called the highest form of human being. But they are not the stuff of which drama is made. Shakespeare could do nothing with Octavius.

Six months before he died, Julius Caesar had altered his will, making Octavius his heir in the first degree and adopting him post-humously as his son. This meant that if Octavius accepted his inheritance, as in fact he did, he inherited the leadership of Caesar's Popular Party, which was the key to political power in Rome, together with the immense party funds left by Julius, out of which he was bound to pay huge legacies to the citizens of Rome. But Mark Antony, no doubt instigated by Fulvia, did not wait to hear what was in the will; he rushed at once, before Caesar's body was cold, to the Temple of Ops and seized the party funds, which the dictator had entrusted to the priests for custody. He even persuaded Caesar's widow, Calpurnia, while prostrate from the blow of her husband's death, to hand over a substantial amount of his private fortune into his, Antony's, allegedly safe keeping.

Cleopatra soon returned to Alexandria, but she stayed long enough in Rome to witness this beginning of the conflict that was to culminate thirteen years later at Actium. On which side were her sympathies likely to lie? It is scarcely conceivable that they could remain neutral in this conflict for the succession to her late master's domain. Would she back the usurper or the legitimate heir; the man who was trying to thwart Caesar's will, or the man who was trying to carry it out; the soldier who had twice proved himself in office an incompetent administrator, or the young man who had the qualities of a great ruler but was the world's worst soldier? Would she, in short, prefer brawn or brains, Goliath or David?

There is no doubt whatever in my mind as to which she would have chosen, and I submit that the evidence is fully consistent with my contention that she actually supported young Caesar Octavianus (as he became by adoption) right from the beginning. He was six years younger than she was - a difference not so great as to rule out sympathy with the boy who, like herself at exactly the same age, found himself pitchforked into a stinking morass of political corruption and intrigue where he was striving with courage, dignity, and patience to secure his legal rights and to fulfil worthily the role that his adoptive father had assigned to him.

Young Caesar and Mark Antony patched-up their quarrel sufficiently to form, with Lepidus, the Second Triumvirate, and to fight together at Philippi, where they disposed of the last vestiges of republican resistance. It was then agreed between them that Antony should take the East, to re-establish Roman dominion in Asia, while Caesar took the West, where

150

he had the more difficult task of restoring Italy's shattered economy and settling huge numbers of time-expired veterans on other people's lands.

Antony began his tour of Asia in typical style. I quote from Langhorne's translation of Plutarch: "When he had enriched himself with the wealth of the country; when his house was the resort of obsequious kings, and queens contended for his favour by their beauty and munificence; then, whilst Caesar was harassed with seditions at Rome, Antony once more gave up his soul to luxury, and fell into all the dissipation of his former life ... the harpers and the pipers, Metrodorus the dancer, the whole corps of the Asiatic drama, who far outdid in buffoonery the poor wretches of Italy; these were the people of the court, the folks that carried all before them. In short, all was riot and disorder.

"When Antony entered Ephesus, women in the dress of Bacchanal and men and boys habited like Pan and the satyrs, marched before him. Nothing was to be seen through the whole city but ivy crowns, and spears wreathed with ivy, harps, flutes and pipes, while Antony was hailed by the name of Bacchus - Bacchus ever kind and free! And such indeed he was to some; but to others he was savage and severe. He deprived many noble families of their fortunes and bestowed them on sycophants and parasites ... He gave his cook the estate of a Magnesian citizen for dressing on supper to his taste.

Antony was ignorant of many things that were transacted under his authority; not that he was indolent, but unsuspecting. He had a simplicity in his nature without much penetration. But when he found that faults had been committed, he expressed the greatest concern and acknowledgement to the sufferers. He was prodigal in his rewards, and severe in his punishments; but the excess was rather in the former than in the latter ..."

Plutarch goes on: "Such was the frail, the flexible Antony, when the love of Cleopatra came in to the completion of his ruin. This awakened every dormant vice, inflamed every guilty passion, and totally extinguished the gleams of remaining virtue..."

It was when he was in Ephesus that Antony sent a message to Cleopatra, ordering her to meet him in Cilicia to answer a charge against her that she had given help to Cassius and the Republicans in the campaign before Philippi.

The receipt of that message must surely have evoked a poignant memory in Cleopatra's mind. Once again an imperious summons to appear before a Roman general to plead her cause. She, the queen of the oldest kingdom in the world, treated like a common citizen of upstart Rome. But she had not the armed force to resist, and she had no wish to see those brutal legionaries marching with their spears - ivy or no ivy - through the streets of Alexandria to establish their drunken general in her palace by force of arms.

Once again, she countered with a stratagem perfectly designed for the conquest of the man she recognised as her enemy. No humble Operation Carpet this time; but something magnificent, befitting her present stature. Something on an Olympic scale - *Operation Venus*. If Antony fancied himself as Bacchus, very well, Cleopatra would be Venus, the Roman equivalent of Isis. The God of Wine would be conquered and enslaved by the Goddess of Love.

As before, the utmost secrecy was maintained during the preparations to ensure complete surprise. Antony had ordered her to appear before him in the market place in Tarsus, where he would be holding his court. Cleopatra did not acknowledge this order, but countered with a request that she might have the pleasure of his company at dinner on board her royal yacht on the evening of her arrival.

She did not hasten over her journey to Tarsus. He waited

Cleopatra and Antony
From a large silver coin issued in Syria in c.34 BC

153

impatiently. At last she appeared like a goddess from heaven, wafted divinely along the river Cydnus in a boat the like of which has never been seen before or since. The stern was overlaid with gold, with purple sails outspread, and oars of silver moving in time to the music flutes, pipes, and harps. The Queen herself, all but naked, reclined under a canopy embroidered with gold of exquisite workmanship, while naked boys like painted Cupids stood fanning her on either side. On the helm and by the rigging beautiful girls were posed in tableaux representing Nereids and the three Graces. As the vessel passed along the river the fragrance of burning incense was wafted to either shore where a vast multitude of people assembled to see the marvellous spectacle.

The entire population of the city had left their shops and homes and businesses. The busy market place was of a sudden deserted, and Antony was left alone on the tribunal. The word had spread that Venus had come to feast with Bacchus for the benefit of Asia.

When Antony recognised the futility of expecting Cleopatra to appear before the tribunal, he sent a message commanding her to dine with him. But Cleopatra insisted that he dine with her. It was a battle of wills, and Cleopatra won. Her victory was never for a moment in doubt.

The next evening the same thing happened. She refused his invitation and insisted on his dining with her. This time preparations were made not for a dinner *à deux* but for a banquet. The barge was lit by myriads of coloured lights which moved in marvellous patterns; sumptuous viands were served on plates of gold encrusted with jewels which the guests were invited to take with them as gifts; and the floor of the banqueting room was covered one foot deep in rose petals. It was not till the third night that the Queen of Egypt consented to accept the Roman general's hospitality. Though he laid on a feast that was magnificent by any normal standards, he felt bound to apologise for its poverty and boorishness compared with hers.

It goes without saying that Cleopatra's success in the battle of the dinner table was followed up each night by a further encounter on her favourite battleground, the bed. Her victory was complete. From this time forward, Mark Antony was her slave.

Now there are several significant differences between a war which is waged, as this one was, between a man and a woman in the socio-sexual field and one that is waged by men against men in the orthodox way with weapons that kill. One difference is that, whereas an enemy who has been decisively beaten in a killing war can be expected to stay down, if not for good, at least for a considerable time, and will be wary of provoking a further encounter, one who has been defeated in a sex war is apt to enjoy the experience and will come back not once but many times, thirsting for further doses of the same medicine. This has its dangers for the victor, because eventually the effect wears off. It is, therefore, important for one who desires to keep her victim captive not to let him become immunised by too frequent repetitions of the same performance.

Cleopatra was fully alive to this danger. Having conquered Antony, she now had to keep him in subjection, partly in order to rob him of the effective mastery of Egypt and the East to which he was entitled by the superior force of his legions, and partly in order to prevent him from interfering while young Caesar was building up his very tenuous position in Rome. Cleopatra never worked so hard in her life as she now did in the winter of 41-40 to keep Mark Antony in thrall. The level of extravagant living in Alexandria that winter reached an all-time high. A society was formed known as *The Society of the Inimitable Life*, whose members took it in turns to lay on entertainments of a kind and on a scale alike inimitable. Besides eating, drinking, and making love on a gargantuan scale, they

155

invented all manner of games, went hunting, fishing, gambling, and gallivanting through the town by night, visiting the high spots and the low spots, with Antony disguised no doubt as a Roman business man and Cleopatra as his slave girl or even - who knows? - a common tart. She suited the style of her conversation to his, guffawed at his bawdy jokes and acquired a vocabulary of obscenities that would have enabled her to hold her own in a swearing match with any foul-mouthed Roman trooper. Never for a moment was Antony allowed to be bored.

While Mark Antony was thus frittering away his time in Alexandria, young Caesar was working hard and establishing for himself a position of strength in Rome. Cleopatra, kept informed by the Egyptian secret service, the best in the world, watched his every move. Antony's brother Lucius was consul in 41, and he and Fulvia did everything in their power to thwart Caesar's efforts to carry out the tasks assigned to him as Triumvir. But Caesar was not to be thwarted. An armed conflict developed in which Caesar's forces were for the first time commanded by his college friend and companion Marcus Vipsanius Agrippa. Agrippa soon had the enemy's forces under siege in Perusia from where Lucius Antony and Fulvia sent urgent entreaties to Mark Antony to come and save them. I suspect - though there is no evidence for this - that Cleopatra saw to it either that the messages did not reach Antony, or, if they did, that they reached him when he was drunk or otherwise engaged in circumstances such that she could be sure his response would be negative.

At all events Mark Antony did not move; Caesar won the war in Italy, and Fulvia and Lucius Antony fled to Greece, where Fulvia died soon after. A little latter, when news reached Mark Antony the Parthians were once again causing trouble in the East, Cleopatra made no attempt to prevent him from setting off to deal with them, but rather urged him on. She could not keep up the strain of the Inimitable Life for ever; a campaign against the Parthians would keep Antony out of Caesar's way, and there was always a chance that he might not come back alive.

On his way to Asia, Antony was diverted to Italy by the news from that quarter. He landed at Brindisi in September 40, where a treaty was signed with Caesar which divided the world once again between Antony in the East, Caesar in the West, and Lepidus, the third member of the Triumvirate, in North Africa. To set a seal on what Caesar this time hoped would be a lasting alliance, he gave his newly widowed sister Octavia in marriage to Antony.

If Cleopatra's dominating motive had been a passionate love for Antony we might have expected some reaction from her when she heard of his intention to marry Octavia while she herself was pregnant with twins by him; but history (as distinct from Shakespeare) records not so much as a squeak from Alexandria. So long as peace prevailed between the two rivals Cleopatra kept quiet. It was when war threatened between them that she took an active part to make sure that the right side won - and the right side for her was *not* Mark Antony's.

There is one revealing episode recorded by Plutarch about this time. Antony was a superstitious man and employed a soothsayer to advise him on his fortunes. The man, be it noted, was an Egyptian. He told Antony that the star of his fortune, though glorious in itself, was obscured by Caesar's and he advised him by all means to keep at the greatest distance from that young man. "The genius of your life," said the soothsayer, "is afraid of Caesar's: when it is alone it stands upright and fearless but when his approaches, yours is dejected and depressed."

In the technique of psychological warfare whereby one artful combatant prepares his opponent's mind for eventual defeat, the modern world could still learn something from Cleopatra. Like the high priestess that she was, she was preparing her victim for the sacrifice.

Antony and Cleopatra did not meet again for three years, in the autumn of 37 when Antony was planning once more to set off on a campaign against the Parthians. She met him in Antioch. He needed Egyptian money to finance his campaign and she made him pay a high price for her support. He bestowed on her the sovereignty of Phoenicia, Coele-Syria, Cyprus, a large part of Cilicia, and parts of Judaea. These gifts that she extracted from Antony have been used as evidence of Cleopatra's insatiable lust for power, but I suggest she had a more subtle motive, or rather, two more subtle motives.

In the first place, the coming struggle between Antony and Caesar was never far from her thoughts, and it was vital to the plan that was already taking shape in her mind that she, not Antony, must be the titular sovereign and supreme ruler of the forces under their command. He was to be her general; and when she gave him an order there must be no question of his not obeying it on the instant.

Secondly, the more territory that she could add to the Egyptian crown, the stronger would be her position *vis-a-vis* Caesar when the time came for her to bargain with him. Caesar had as yet no inkling of her attitude or her plan. He played his cards very close to his chest, and she could not altogether trust him to react the way she wanted when at last he knew that far from being, as he thought, his enemy, she was in fact and had been all along, his secret ally.

Antony had, of course, no right to give away provinces which belonged to the Senate and People of Rome, but this did not bother Cleopatra. There was, however, one territory she particularly wanted to acquire which Antony could not give her. This was Judaea. Caesar and Antony, acting for

158

once in concert with the backing of the Senate, had very recently recognised Herod as King of Judaea; and Herod was not a man to be lightly persuaded to transfer his allegiance to the Queen of Egypt. Nevertheless, Antony did give her, over Herod's head, the balsam groves of Jericho - a not inappropriate gift considering that they were the main source of raw materials for the perfume industry on which she so heavily depended.

Having seen Antony off on his Parthian expedition, Cleopatra returned from Antioch and paid a visit to Jerusalem on the way. Now, Herod was the wiliest potentate in the Orient, and a firm supporter of the power of Rome as personified in Mark Antony, on whose legions he relied in the last resort to maintain his hold on his by no means docile Jewish subjects. Cleopatra, having failed to get Antony to grant her the sovereignty of Judaea, decided she must detach Herod from his allegiance to Antony in some other way. Adopting her customary tactics, she tried to seduce him. The story is told by the Jewish historian, Josephus. Acting as if she had fallen passionately in love with her attractive young host, she deployed her incomparable expertise in the art of seduction to entice him into her bed.

But for once, Cleopatra had met her match. Herod was too wary a bird to fall into the trap. He had watched with admiration the success of her technique with Antony, and sensed that she was now trying it on him in order to discredit him with the Roman general. She was out - he was certain of it - to ruin Antony, and he was determined to stop her if he could. But he knew both the simple trusting nature of the Roman and the strength of the spell that Cleopatra had cast upon him. There was not the slightest chance of his being able to convince Antony that the woman he, Antony, adored was planning to destroy him. So he turned to the only other way that seemed open to him to save his cause. He planned to do her in. She would not be the first person that he had murdered. But, he reflected (and his advisers ultimately persuaded him to this effect) she would almost certainly be the last. Mark Antony's wrath on hearing the news of the queen's death would know no bounds, and his revenge would be terrible.

So the Queen of Egypt's visit to Herod the Great ended in a stalemate, with the honours slightly in her favour - for she did at least get him to agree to pay her an annual rent for the balsam groves of Jericho. On her departure he escorted her to the frontier with punctilious ceremony, gifts were exchanged, and no doubt public statements were issued to the effect that there had been a useful exchange of views between the two sovereigns on matters of mutual interest.

Passing over the ensuing years which witnessed the failure of Antony's campaign against the Parthians, his divorce of Octavia, Caesar's initial defeats and eventual success in his war with Sextus Pompey, and his elimination of his ally Lepidus who turned traitor on him, we come now to the last act of the drama.

It began in 34 when Antony returned from the East where, after a major defeat at the hands of the King of Parthia, he saved his face by successfully belabouring the harmless King of Armenia. This victory deserved, he considered, a Roman Triumph. This, however, was not accorded him by the Senate in Rome, but by the Queen of Egypt in Alexandria. Cleopatra made sure that it was she, not Antony, who got the honours. At a spectacular ceremony in the market place, seated on golden thrones, Cleopatra was proclaimed Queen of Kings, and her thirteen-year-old son, Caesarion, King of Kings and co-regent with his mother. Under this supreme sovereignty, Cleopatra and Caesarion were proclaimed specifically rulers of Egypt, Cyprus and Coele-Syria, while the remaining territories were divided between the three children which she had by Antony. Antony himself got nothing. He was made Imperator, her general, but nothing more.

Not unnaturally, the Roman Senate refused to recognise these arrangements. An intense war of propaganda followed between the friends of Antony and those of Caesar. The atmosphere in Rome became so charged that Domitius Ahenobarbus, consul for the year 32, one of Julius Caesar's murderers and now a supporter of Antony, deemed it prudent at the beginning of his consulship to leave the city. Accompanied by about 300 senators he fled to Antony who had his headquarters at Ephesus.

Domitius was an able and determined man whose plan, no doubt, was to get Antony to muster a host in the East and descend on Italy by sea and land before Caesar had time to organise its defence. If such an attack had been launched in the spring of 32 it is a fair probability that, given reasonable generalship, Antony would have carried all before him; for Caesar's forces were weary, the economy was impoverished by war, and Roman strength on the home front was at a low ebb.

Inspired by Domitius, Antony issued a general proclamation calling on the whole of the East to rise in arms against Caesar. This was a situation fraught with the utmost danger to Cleopatra's Grand Design. She reacted instantly with characteristic resource and audacity. The first to answer Mark Antony's call, she hurried off to Ephesus with a fleet of 200 ships, an immense supply of gold, and provisions for the whole army. There, vaunting no doubt her title of Queen of Kings and ignoring the fact that she had no military training or experience, Cleopatra coolly assumed the supreme command of the entire expedition and proceeded to treat Antony as her Chief of Staff. The expedition amounted in the end to a vast force of some 800 ship and half a million men - the mightiest armada ever to have been assembled in one place. Amongst those who joined it with their forces were kings and princes of Cilicia,

161

Cappadocia, Paphlagonia, Pontus, Galatia, Commagene, Emesa, Thrace, Mauritania, Arabia and Media.

One king was conspicuously absent - Herod of Judaea. Cleopatra did not want *him* around, so with the help of a friendly Arab King she had cooked up a war for him on the southern borders of Judaea and persuaded Antony that it was more important that Herod should fight the Arabs there than join him in fighting Caesar. Herod was doubtless glad to be out of it. He must have seen that he did not stand a chance with Antony against Cleopatra's perfumed presence, and he proceeded accordingly to lay off his bets and prepare for Caesar's victory. This he did so successfully that Caesar in due course confirmed him in his kingdom, thus enabling him to earn immortal fame for himself as the chief villain in a very different drama thirty years later.

Domitius and his friends must have viewed Cleopatra's arrival with dismay. He himself flatly refused to acknowledge her title, and addressed her simply by her name. Whether or not they suspected her loyalty to their cause, they all sensed disaster if she stayed and they tried their utmost to induce her to go home. Antony himself added his entreaties, but she was adamant. At length his friends in Rome became so alarmed that they sent a certain Geminius to open Antony's eyes to his danger and "to put him", as Plutarch has it, "on his guard against the abrogation of his power." But Cleopatra managed to prevent Geminius from getting an audience alone with Antony. At dinner she put him as far away from the general as possible.

But at length Geminius did succeed in attracting Antony's attention at dinner, when the latter was already in his cups. Asked what he was doing there, Geminius answered that one part of the reason could only be communicated to Antony when he was sober, but the other part was all too obvious. "If only," he said, "Cleopatra would return to Egypt, all would be well."

162

Quick as a flash came Cleopatra's deadly riposte. "You have done well, Geminius," she said, "to confess without having to be put to the torture." Thus in one sentence she demolished his credibility by making out that he was a paid agent of Caesar's, and at the same time so put the fear of God into the unhappy man that he took the next ship back to Rome.

The queen's first objective now was to play for time. This she did in classic Cleopatran style. The headquarters of the armada were moved to the island of Samos, where she kept Antony's mind occupied with every kind of thought except the thought of war. Kings and princes were challenged to vie with her and with one another in the lavishness and originality of their entertainments. The whole East was drained of actors and actresses, musicians, jugglers and entertainers of all kinds who flocked to Samos to amuse the richest audience in the world. "While the rest of the world," says Plutarch, "was venting its anguish in groans and tears, that island alone was piping and dancing."

So passed the summer of BC. 32, and the following winter. The next spring Cleopatra, still anxious to delay, deemed nevertheless that it was expedient to make a move in the direction of Italy; so the headquarters were moved to Athens. Here a new round of parties was commenced, and a brilliant ceremony was held at which the Queen of Kings was invested with the highest honours by the world's first democracy. Special coins were struck for the occasion by the Athenian people depicting her in the guise of the goddess Isis.

Thus did Cleopatra give Caesar the time that he badly needed to build up his forces in Italy. She also used the time to put Antony through a final course of rehearsals in the part she had assigned to him to play - that of her subordinate commander, so disciplined that he could be relied on to obey without hesitation when she gave the fateful command "Follow me". For a woman blessed as she was with a voluptuous body and a melodious voice which she could use to pour forth either the sweetest honey or the purest vitriol as easily as you or I turn on the hot or cold taps in our baths, the conditioning of a man of Mark Antony's simple and sensual nature by rewards and punishments must have been child's play. She made him always refer to her in public as his sovereign and sent him love letters in jewelled envelopes which he had to read at once, even though he were engaged in conclave with kings and tetrarchs. On one occasion when he was judging a case in the forum she beckoned to him as she passed by in her litter, and he promptly went off to join her, leaving one of the foremost advocates of the day high and dry in the middle of a speech.

At last, in the spring of 31, Caesar was ready. By overwhelming majorities the Senate and the popular Assembly passed resolutions declaring a state of war. The declared enemy was not Antony but Cleopatra. It was war between the Roman people and the Queen of Egypt - no one else. Mark Antony's name was not mentioned.

Historians have cited this calculated omission as an example of young Caesar's astuteness, for by it he gave every Roman in Antony's army the chance to come over to the other side without appearing to be disloyal. Personally, I take it as the first evidence of active collusion between Cleopatra and Caesar. If Antony's name had been bracketed with hers in the Senate's declaration as everyone expected, Demitius and his friends would have been given just the lever they wanted for insisting that Mark Antony's authority as commander was at least equal to Cleopatra's; and that was precisely what Cleopatra wanted to avoid. There are other signs of collusion too. In fact, it can be said that from this point on all the moves made by the two protagonists fitted together in an extraordinarily apposite way to produce the end result, namely a total victory for Caesar with the minimum number of casualties and an almost complete absence of the hatred, humiliation, and bitterness that are the normal aftermath of defeat in war.

A considerable number of Antony's supporters - not only Roman citizens - now began to desert what they felt to be a sinking ship. Cleopatra, by putting on a haughty and overbearing manner, did her best to speed the exodus. Titius and Plancus, two ex-consuls, could brook her insults no longer and went over to Caesar. Dellius, one of Antony's most valuable aides, did the same. 2,000 Galatian cavalry changed sides; and at last the redoubtable Domitius himself acknowledged defeat and deserted. Antony and Cleopatra sent his baggage after him. An Arab prince and a Roman senator were unhappily caught in the act of desertion, and Antony had them executed. This stopped the rot for the time being.

From the outset, the initiative in the war was taken and held by Caesar and his general Agrippa. Antony and Cleopatra seem to have had no clear idea of what they were trying to do until they found themselves blockaded by the enemy on the west coast of Greece. All they *could* do then was to try to get out. Their forces were superior in numbers but their generalship was appalling. They were reported to be engaged day after day in violent quarrels. Antony was still a good soldier who, given the sole command, might have led his forces to a resounding victory, but he could not get his Commander-in-Chief to see military sense, and in desperation he took more heavily than ever to the bottle.

The critical issue arose over the question whether, in order to break out of the blockade, they should attack Caesar's land forces or his fleet. Antony and his generals, supported by strong military arguments, favoured the former course. Cleopatra alone favoured the latter. Hers was the final decision, and she decided accordingly to fight by sea.

This was the decision that suited Caesar. The tactics he now adopted in the sea fight were designed to suit her. Antony's fleet was drawn up with his main force, consisting of heavy ships of war, stretched in a line in front of the entrance to the Gulf of Ambracia, on one side of which is the promontory of Actium. Cleopatra with her Egyptian squadron was in the rear of the centre of the line, right in the narrows at the entrance to the Gulf. Agrippa drew up his fleet of lighter, faster ships in line opposite Antony's some distance away.

For some time nothing happened. Then the squadrons on the two flanks of Caesar's line moved outwards, as if to outflank Antony's. Antony was forced to open out his line, leaving gaps between his ships in the centre. In the general engagement which followed, neither side had the advantage. It was then that Cleopatra and her sixty ships hoisted sail, burst through one of the gaps causing confusion as they went, reached the open sea and set course for home. Antony followed; and the war was lost and won.

Almost any manoeuvre on Caesar's part other than the one he adopted must have resulted in the Egyptian ships staying bottled up in the entrance to the gulf or having to fight their way out. Considering that Cleopatra in her treasure ship was the greatest prize of all, why did Caesar not concentrate his effort on trying to capture her? He not merely allowed her, he positively invited her to escape. We can safely assume that on this occasion, as always, he had a good reason for what he did. The only satisfactory explanation is that the whole thing was prearranged.

The fantastic strain of the last few weeks took its toll on Cleopatra's nerves. For two days she lay exhausted in her cabin, unable to bring herself to face the man she had loved, and ruined. But somehow in the end she managed it, and near-normal relations were gradually restored between them.

She now had two problems on her hands. First, how to dispose of Mark Antony himself, and second, how to induce Caesar to accept the role she had assigned to him of King of

Kings and reign with her over a united world.

As for Antony, why, it may be asked, did she not simply kill him? She could have done so at any time and saved a vast amount of trouble. The answer is that she knew the Roman character too well. Romans, however much they hated one another, always stuck together in the face of foreigners. Had Cleopatra killed Antony, she herself would have been put to death by young Caesar as surely as Pompey's murderers had been executed by his father Julius.

Nevertheless, in the days of mounting tension before the battle there is evidence that she did actually plan to murder Antony. Dellius, his aide, was convinced of this and had reported to Antony accordingly. And Pliny records how Cleopatra put poison in Antony's cup at dinner one night just before the battle. She carried it in a flower in her hair. But as Antony raised the cup to his lips she seized it from him. Evidently she lost her resolution at the last moment. Her lame excuse, which history as well as Antony had to accept for want of a better, was that she wanted to prove to him that his personal security service was incompetent. This does not ring true. If an American President's wife wanted to prove that her husband's security men were no good, would she establish her point by demonstrating how easy it was for *her* to put arsenic in his coffee?

Back in Alexandria after the battle, Cleopatra concentrated on trying to get Antony to kill himself. They made a suicide pact together, and spent many hours trying out various kinds of poison to find out which was the quickest and the least painful. Remembering the happy times they had had together ten years before, they now formed another society, this time called the *Society of Companions in Death*. Such was her irrepressible gaiety that Cleopatra laughed in the face of Death himself.

By all the rules Antony should have fallen on his sword in

the moment of defeat; but he still wanted to live, and she was forced to put up a show of resistance with him for the defence of Egypt. Her betrayal of him now became almost blatant when she gave him troops to command at the frontier, and at the same time ordered them secretly to surrender to Caesar. Even the gullible Antony began to suspect, but he still could not and would not believe that the woman he worshipped was betraying him.

Were his eyes at last opened, perhaps, at the very end when he found that she had tricked him even at the moment of death by a false report that she had already killed herself in her monument? Or was his faith once more restored by the manifestation of love that she bore him, and her frantic distress when she and a handmaid strained themselves to pull his heavy, dying body up onto the roof of the monument, there to cradle him on her bosom as he expired? That she really loved him was proved by her dying wish that she be buried in his grave. Surely no Christian saint ever obeyed more faithfully than Cleopatra the injunction: Love your enemies.

But what of Caesar? How that young man must have dreaded his inevitable meeting with the queen he had defeated, but who was yet victorious. Her will had conquered Mark Antony as it had conquered Julius Caesar before him, and now she was poised for her final conquest over him. What would she say to him? What would he say to her?

After Actium Caesar had taken nine long months to make his unhurried progress through the east, settling the affairs of nations as he went, before reaching the frontier of Egypt. During this time a double correspondence took place in which open letters were sent accompanied by secret messages. At one point Cleopatra revealed her hand completely. Unknown to Antony she sent Caesar a messenger bearing gifts. Caesar accepted the gifts but sent no reply to the invitation they were intended to convey - an invitation to become a king. The gifts were gifts she had never offered to Antony: a crown, a sceptre, and a throne.

Cleopatra was an incurable romantic, but Caesar was a stern realist. Fourteen years of unrelenting struggle against corruption, injustice, treachery and every kind of evil had turned him from a callow youth into a man of indomitable will, harder than the hardest steel.

We do not know what took place at their one and only interview. The historians, of course, have told us, but they were not there. No one else was there; and of all the famous people in history none were greater masters in the art of keeping secrets to themselves than Caesar Augustus and Queen Cleopatra. Not for nothing did Augustus choose as his personal emblem the image of the Egyptian Sphinx.

As usual, luck was on Caesar's side - a sure sign of the continued favour of the gods. Cleopatra, showing once again her unerring insight into the weaknesses of the man she had to deal with, sensed that what Caesar wanted was not her love but her gold. He needed it desperately to pay his war debts. Her plan - a typically theatrical plan - was to wall herself up in the mausoleum she had specially built to contain herself and all her treasures, to bargain with him through a grille, and threaten that if he would not agree to her terms, she would take poison and set the whole thing alight. But for once her plan went wrong. Two of Caesar's men got in by a trick and took her prisoner. She tried to stab herself but the dagger was snatched from her, and she was submitted to the supreme indignity of having her clothing searched by a Roman soldier for other means of self-destruction.

She had now nothing left to bargain with but herself. For the first and last time in her life she appeared as a suppliant, pleading not for herself but for her children and her people. We can believe the historians when they tell us that her acting was superb. According to Dio Cassius, Cleopatra, dressed in

169

mourning garb, surrounded by images of Julius Caesar and carrying a packet of his letters clasped to her bosom, combined a matchless display of grieving widowhood with a passionate plea to young Caesar to fill his father's place in her now empty heart. But Caesar, fearful of succumbing to her charm, kept his eyes on the ground and merely promised that she should come to no harm, though in fact he was intending to take her captive to Rome for his triumph. Such is Dio's account; but I do not believe it. Caesar's character, like Cleopatra's, has been grossly misrepresented by history.

When Julius Caesar was murdered in 44 BC many people must have noticed how strangely similar were the circumstances of his death to those which had surrounded the murder three hundred years earlier of Philip of Macedon. Like Caesar, Philip was a great warrior who was slain at the height of his power, after he had consolidated his rule at home and when he was on the point of setting off for a campaign in the East. But Philip's murder was not the end of that story. It was only the beginning. Philip had a young son, Alexander, who took up his father's inheritance and went on to found an empire. Surely this was an omen for Caesar's young son, Octavius. Octavius accepted his adoptive father's inheritance not because he wanted it - for he was something of a coward by nature - but because he felt it was his duty, seeing that civil war was certain to break out if he refused, and because he believed himself called by a Divine will to follow in the footsteps of Alexander the Great and found an empire. Who will say that he was wrong? Had not a fortune-teller once told him that he was destined to rule the world? And when he entered Rome after the dictator's murder had not Apollo welcomed him by putting a halo round the sun? Gods speak in omens to those who believe in omens.

Cleopatra, too, must have seen the parallel between the fortune of Octavius and the founder of her own dynasty, and been encouraged thereby to foster the dream of a revival of Alexander's empire. But whereas the empire she dreamed of would have its capital in Alexander's own city in Egypt, young Caesar planned from the beginning that his would be a Roman Empire. He planned to build it so that it would endure far longer than Alexander's. Its capital would be Rome; and in Rome there was no place for kings and queens.

He himself, now 33, was already married to his second wife, Livia; but even if he had been free and willing to ally himself with the Queen of Egypt, it was politically impossible for him to do so. The events of the last few years had turned Cleopatra's name into an abomination in Roman ears. Such was the people's hatred of this sorceress who had bewitched two of their favourite idols that they were now thirsting for her blood.

Somehow he had to disillusion her. What actual part he offered her in his empire we cannot know, but it was not the part she had bargained for. She had given him the victory, and she had hoped in return to reign with him as Queen of Kings. He accepted the victory, but he made no bargain. The Roman Empire was not for sale.

Cleopatra must have realised early in the interview that her cause was lost. There would be no royal marriage to sanctify the union of East and West, neither in Alexandria nor in Rome. Her pleas must then have been directed to preserving the lives of her children and the freedom of her people.

Caesar not only agreed to spare the lives of Cleopatra's children by Antony but took them back with him to Rome and put them in the care of his sister Octavia, who had been Antony's wife. But Caesarion, her son by Julius Caesar, presented him with a different problem. He himself had acquired the name of Caesar by adoption, and he owed a large part of his success to the magic of that name. He had a daughter by his first wife, but his marriage with Livia was barren. He had to reckon with the possibility that he would have no male heir

171

who could claim to be called Caesar otherwise than by adoption. As the intended founder of an imperial dynasty, young Caesar looked into the future and saw the spectre of future wars if Caesarion lived and had sons bearing that now awesome name. With remorseless logic he decided that the boy must die. To Cleopatra he merely promised that he would consider her plea for his life.

I believe that it was as a result of a promise made during this interview that Augustus never made Egypt a province of the Roman Empire to be governed by a governor like other provinces. Instead, he assumed himself the succession to the throne of the Ptolemies, accepting, in effect, her offer of the kingship, and governed Egypt through a personal Viceroy. The country was taken out of the arena of Roman politics, and no Roman senator was allowed to enter it without a written authority signed by the emperor himself.

Another deducible result of the interview was a pact between Caesar and Cleopatra to keep secret for ever the part she had played in his victory. It was clearly in his interest that the world should believe, and go on believing, that he had won the war by honourable means in a fair fight. Cleopatra for her part had no desire to be known as a traitor. For the peace of the world she had sacrificed her virtue, her honour, and her throne, and the world in return reviled her as a sorceress and a whore. That was enough. Let it be believed that she had at least been loyal to her lovers.

Above all, it was essential in the interest of the peace that both alike had striven for and had at last achieved that their collusion should not be revealed so long as that peace endured. If the facts of Cleopatra's betrayal of the Eastern powers were made public, the East would surely rise up again in anger and seek revenge. Only so long as they could blame their defeat on her incompetent generalship and her cowardice - that is to say, on the fact, as they saw it, of her womanhood - could they

172

accept the consequences with resignation.

At the end of the interview, there was only one thing left for Cleopatra to do. The time had come for her to keep her tryst with Antony. Dressed in the ancient regalia of the pharaohs, with the royal diadem on her head and clasping a serpent, symbol of Egyptian power, to her bosom, the death of the last Queen of Egypt was a fitting end to the magic drama of her life.

True to his promise, Augustus never divulged the secret of his victory. Not only did he not write the full story of his rise to power, but throughout the remaining 44 years of his life he censored every record made by others and deleted from it any reference from which a future historian might have been led to suspect that the whole truth had not been told.

Shortly before he died in A.D. 14, the first Roman emperor gave a hint that he had not forgotten the woman to whom he owed his empire. Now 76, he was resting in his villa on Capri when a happy incident occurred. I quote from Robert Graves' translation of Suetonius:

"As he (Augustus) had sailed through the gulf of Puteoli, the passengers and crew of a recently arrived Alexandrian ship had put on white robes and garlands, burned incense and wished him the greatest of good fortune - which, they said, he certainly deserved, because they owed their lives to him and their liberty to sail the seas; in a word, their entire freedom and prosperity. This incident gratified Augustus so deeply that he gave each member of his staff forty gold pieces, making them promise under oath to spend them only on Alexandrian trade goods..."

I am sure that Augustus acknowledged to himself, if to no one else, the debt which he and the whole world owed to Cleopatra, and that in this unwonted act of generosity he was paying tribute to her memory. If only, he thought, *she* had been here, to hear these Alexandrian people, how happy it would have made her. Their freedom was what she had pleaded for, and freedom was what they now spontaneously acknowledged he had given them.

Evidence that some such thought was in his mind is contained in what followed. I continue the quotation:

"...What was more, he made the last two or three days of his stay in Capri the occasion for distributing among other presents, Roman gowns and Greek cloaks to the islanders; insisting that the Romans should talk Greek and dress like Greeks, and that the Greeks should do the opposite."

This was indeed an appropriately symbolic act for the man who, by his life's work, had created a new world order in which East and West were peaceably united. But Augustus was by nature the most un-theatrical of men. Surely the idea of getting people to dress up was not his own but was inspired by the memory of an actress he had known long ago who adored the fun of dressing up and of seeing other people dressed up too.

The same thought, the Cleopatran thought , that "All the world's a stage and all the men and women merely players" was in his mind when he died a few days later. To a group of friends who were assembled round his deathbed he asked: "Have I played my part worthily in the comedy of life?" And then added the lines with which actors were accustomed to bow themselves off the stage:-

"IF BY MY ACTING I HAVE GIVEN YOU CAUSE FOR PLEASURE, KINDLY GIVE ME YOUR APPLAUSE."

Cleopatra, in the role just described, was a type B character, equally balanced between ambition or desire on the one hand and timidity on the other. Her abundant vitality gave her a passionate love of life which she used to the full to give pleasure to others and to play her own dramatic part in history with courage, endurance, and gaiety.

One thing she desired above all else, not for herself but for all mankind: permanent, universal peace. She worked courageously and indefatigably in pursuit of that goal. For it she sacrificed her comfort, her wealth, her honour, and her life. The world in return requited her with obloquy and hate. In that way would divine justice be likely to have rewarded her after she died?

Born the daughter of a king whose crown she inherited, Cleopatra might have started her next life as a servant girl in an obscure household. Next time round, however, we might expect to find her born again to parents of royal or near-royal blood. Without doubt her vivacity and charm would make an indelible mark on the society that was fortunate enough to know her; and the beauty of her mind would be mirrored in the beauty of the person. Careless of her reputation amongst a respectable bourgeoisie, she might again shock the genteel world by an audacious pursuit of peace and happiness by unconventional means; but in place of the opprobrium that caused her to cut short her colourful life in the Roman world, the Fates might be expected to compensate her with a long life richly rewarded by the world's honour and admiration. Above all, Cleopatra reborn would still be an actress, consciously acting a part on a new world stage.

As a type B character, we would expect Cleopatra's soul to have an orbital period halfway between the As and the Cs, or about 1960 years. From her birth in 69 BC, this would take her to about AD 1892.

In that precise year, 1892, a third daughter was born in

175

London to Violet, Marchioness of Granby, whose husband, the Marquess, succeeded later to the 200-year-old Dukedom of Rutland. The Lady Diana Manners, better known by her married name of Lady Diana Cooper, viscountess Norwich, turned out to be a girl of outstanding beauty and vivacity, and a natural born actress with a strong relish for theatricality.

Born late in the reign of Queen Victoria when the *Pax Britannica* was at its zenith and the English aristocracy was never more secure, Lady Diana could not have enjoyed a childhood more free from the dangers, the anxieties, and the distress that had beset the childhood of Cleopatra. Nor could her life's ending have been more different. She died in 1986 in her ninety-fifth year, having enjoyed universal respect and admiration in a quiet and comfortable old age.

Thanks to the three volumes of her autobiography (1) we have an authentic record of Lady Diana's thoughts and feelings in the many adventures of her eventful life, from which it is possible to construct, as it were, a picture of the contours of her mind for comparison with the picture of Cleopatra's mind portrayed above. Here are a few of the highlights of the two pictures thus drawn, set out in parallel columns.

Cleopatra	Lady Diana
- Her childhood and early youth were disturbed by wars and civil strife;	- Despite the security of her actual circumstances, her childhood and early youth were troubled by groundless fears of improbable disasters;
- Saved Egypt from war with Rome by becoming the mistress successively of the Roman leaders Julius Caesar and Mark Antony;	- In August 1914 expressed a wish to be able to stop World War I (then just begun) by becoming the mistress of the German Kaiser;
- Formed the *Society of the Inimitable Life* in Alexandria in 41-40 BC;	- Formed the *Corrupt Coterie* of young people whose pride it was to be *Unlike-Other-People*(3); Their gay frolics and daring escapades shocked polite society in London and Venice and made headline news in 1913-15;
- After the Battle of Actium, formed the *Society of Companions in Death*;	- After the outbreak of World War I, the young men of the *Coterie* were killed one after another, but the *Coterie* continue under her leadership and its parties became known as the Dances of Death;

- Made a suicide pact with Mark Antony after their defeat at Actium;	- Proposed a suicide pact with her future husband, Duff Cooper, when it seemed that the Allies might be going to be defeated;
- Named her son Julius Caesar 'Caesarion'('Little Caesar');	- Named her only son 'John Julius';
- Acquired a vocabulary of foul language from Antony and his companions in arms;	- Acquired a vocabulary of foul language from wounded soldiers whom she nursed at Guy's Hospital;
- Was criticized for practising liberal sexual morality;	- Was criticized for reputedly practising liberal sexual morality;
- Famed for her wit, audacity and charm, but capable on occasion of withering scorn;	- Famed for her beauty, wit, audacity, and charm but capable on occasion of withering scorn;
- Disguised true intentions by superb acting on real life's stage, which she enlivened by her natural talent for theatrical behaviour;	- Played leading part in Max Reinhardt's stage production of *The Miracle* in Europe and USA, and was acclaimed by a well-known producer as "the finest actress he had ever seen"(4). She needed no rehearsing.

- When taken prisoner by young Caesar's men, she suffered the pain and indignity of being forced to remain standing with her hands above her head;

- Doing physical exercises as a little girl it was found that she could not raise her arms higher than her shoulders;

- Died by her own hand in a theatrical setting, in her 39th year, to avoid being sent to Rome as a prisoner and executed there;

- Died peacefully in her 95th year. The three volumes of her autobiography all bore titles taken from Wordsworth's Ode *Intimations of Immortality*, which contains the following lines:

"Our birth is but a sleep and a forgetting: The Soul that rises with us, our life's Star, Hath had elsewhere its setting."

- Her two closest friends, who died with her, were named Iran or (Iris) and Charmion.

- Her two closest friends were Iris Tree and Katherine Asquith.

179

This list of parallels, coupled with the coincidence of the actual with the calculated birth date, is enough, I suggest, to constitute a good *prima facie* case for saying that the minds of these two remarkable women were one and the same, passing through the world in two different incarnations. The last item but one on the list is of special interest because it indicates how a mental experience in one life can affect a physical trait in another. The classical authors do not expressly say that Cleopatra was made to hold her hands above her head, but that can be assumed from Plutarch's record that when she produced a dagger from under her clothing and tried to kill herself, the Roman officer took the dagger from her and then *'shook her clothes lest she should have poison concealed about her'*. The episode was clearly a traumatic experience for the Queen of Egypt, and it would not be surprising if the trauma took the form of a mental blockage in a later incarnation. When doctors examined Lady Diana as a child they could find no muscular weakness that could account for her inability to raise her harms above her head. All they could do was to prescribe a regime of physical exercises and 'galvanism'. The fact that the defect was eventually cured by these means points to its having been primarily of a psychological nature. But how could a happy little girl of five or six, born into a happy and prosperous family, have acquired a psychological 'hang-up' which inhibited her attempts to raise her arms, unless she had inherited it from a traumatic event experienced in a former life?

Notes on Chapter 12 - Cleopatra

1. Diana Cooper: *The Rainbow Comes and Goes* (1958); *The Light of Common Day* (1959); *Trumpets from the Steep* (1960); Rupert Hart-Davis, London.

2. Diana Cooper: *The Rainbow Comes and Goes*, p.117

3. Ibid., p.82: *"Our pride was to be unafraid of words, unshocked by drink, and unashamed of 'decadence' and gambling - Unlike-Other-People."*

4. Diana Cooper: *The Light of Common Day*, p.29, quoting from a letter written to Duff Cooper by Lord Castlerosse after seeing the first night's production of *The Miracle* in New York in the company of the British producer C.B. Cochran, whose comments on the production he quoted, adding his own enthusiastic eulogies.

APPENDIX I

Names and Numbers

When, inspired by Sir John Sheppard's lecture on *Macbeth* and the *Agamemnon*, I started to collect historical data for other comparisons to support the reincarnation theory, it soon became obvious that there was something seriously wrong with that part of the theory which required one to look for the rebirth of a great personality either after a half orbit of five or six centuries or after a full orbit of ten or twelve. The historical evidence of reincarnation, taken all together, was overwhelming, but there were serious discrepancies in the timing of the rebirths. I decided to analyse these discrepancies by plotting on a graph the orbital periods revealed by the evidence against 'mean birth dates', i.e., dates calculated as the half-way points in time between the first and second births. The results in respect of all the pairs of lives of which the *full* orbits are identified in the preceding pages are reproduced in Appendices II and III below.

The graph confirms at least one part of the theory, namely that which states that thinkers, poets, and artists tend to have shorter orbits than soldiers and statesmen. Apart from the maverick case of Socrates/Darwin, which I dealt with in the text (p.67), the outstanding exception is no.9, the Gracchi/ Simon Bolivar combination, which I put in the men-of-action category (Type A) because of Bolivar's great military and political achievements. By nature however he (like the Gracchi) was more of an idealist and a constitution-maker than a soldier-statesman, and he ought perhaps, therefore, to be classed among the thinkers (Type C).

The graph reveals a broad pattern of orbital periods increasing up to a maximum of about 2100 years at mean date A.D. 700 (spanning the years from, say, 350 B.C. to A.D. 1750), and then falling to 1960 years for persons born about 70 B.C. and reborn at the end of the 19th century. I hope that one day someone will be able to expalin in precise mathematical terms the reason why these changes should have occurred, and thence go on to predict the future course of 'next-life expectations'.

One other conclusion - a very unexpected one - resulted from the compilation of these tables.

I first noticed that the name HANNIBAL had much in common with IBRAHIM. The letters are arranged in a different order, but with one vowel change (A into I), and with the consonant L regarded as interchangeable with its phonetic partner R, and likewise N with M, they are the same.

It then appeared that the name HAMILCAR had a similar affinity with MOHAMMED ALI. Allowing for other vowel changes and the interchangeability of other pairs of consonants such as P and B, F and V, D and T, it then transpired that in a substantial number of other cases men who had made their names great in ancient times had somehow managed to retain echoes of those names when they were born into the modern world. Thus SULLA (pronounced to rhyme with 'fuller') FELIX is recognisably echoed in ROOSEVELT. Other echoes are found in:

PERICLES	-	CHURCHILL
ALCIBIADES	-	PETROV son of ALEXEI
AESCHYLUS	-	SHAKE-
ARISTOPHANES	-	SPEARE
ARISTOCLES (PLATO)	-	DESCARTES
PHILIPPOS	-	NAPOLEON
CAESAR	-	CHURCHILL
MARCUS ANTONIUS	-	KEMAL
MARIUS	-	MAX AITKEN
CATILINA	-	MUSSOLINI
HORATIUS	-	HOUSMAN
DAVID	-	OCTAVIUS
ADOLF HITLER	-	AEMILIUS LEPIDUS

Considered individually these coincidences are not convin-cing and every one of them could be regarded as an insignificant accident of chance. But taken together the evidence of a causal connection underlying them cannot be lightly dismissed. The coincidences in the names of the two North African generals MOHAMMED ALI and IBRAHIM with HAMILCAR and HANNIBAL are significant in themselves, whilst the total number in the Table is too great to be accounted for by random chance. (This can be tested by comparing two lists of names chosen from Classical and modern European history respectively, and pairing them at random.)

Place names, too, may have echoes that reverberate across the centuries between one life and another. It was surely such an echo, not just a chance coincidence, that guided Ibrahim in his campaign in Turkey to choose the town of KONIA near which to re-enact the famous victory he had won two thousand years earlier against the Romans at CANNAE.

Plato in his myth described how the souls of the departed on returning to this world have to choose their new lives from a variety of many different kinds offered them by the Fates.

In other words, we choose our own mothers and fathers to whom to be born. This is not as irrational as it may sound. Whether the decision be made consciously or unconsciously, there have to be reasons why a given psyche approaching the time of rebirth should be attracted to enter one mother's womb rather than another's; and it is not unreasonable to suppose that among the factors which might help to determine that decision the sound of a name could well be not the least important.

In antiquity people commonly believed that some names possessed magical powers. In the Egyptian myth the goddess Isis acquired her power to perform miracles by discovering the secret name of the sungod Ra. And in the history of the Jews the name of Yahweh was made so formidable by the miracles performed by Moses that even the priests did not dare to pronounce it aloud lest by doing so they should invoke those formidable powers against themselves. This ancient awe of awe-inspiring names is deeply ingrained in our subconscious minds, and it sometimes comes to the surface in the conscious minds of children. This is explicable in terms of the reincarnation process.

The life force has a liquid quality that enables it to adapt itself to any shape of body as water adapts itself to the shape of any container. In life the body keeps the psyche separate from its neighbours; but in death there is no body to perform that function, and one psyche, like a raindrop, can divide into two, or two can interpenetrate one another and come back as one. In these circumstances a name, which is a mental entity independent of the body, may take on the body's function of keeping the psyche whole and separate. It is natural, therefore, that the soul of a man who has made a great name for himself in a certain walk of life should cherish that name in death and, on returning to earth to live again, should seek to invest himself with the nearest equivalent name that can be found in his new environment.

The fact that the order of the letters and syllables of the new names in many of these cases is different from the order of the corresponding parts of the old names - e.g. Hannibal / Ibrahim - tells us something about the geometry of the reincarnation process.

Time in this world is uni-dimensional. All the events of our lives take place in a strict chronological sequence. We can no more change that sequence than we could change the order of the places we would have to pass through on a train journey on a certain route, say from Paris to Moscow. That same unalterable sequence governs the order of the sounds or letters in a person's name so long as they are alive. Our theory, however, holds that in death the psyche enters a realm where time has more than one dimension. It is no longer purely linear, and there is no fixed immutability about sequences of events, or about the order of syllables in a name. It is as if our trans-Europe express has taken wings and, looking down from the air onto the two-dimensional map of the land below, we can visit any place, on or off the route, in whatever order we happen to prefer.

Once back on Earth, however, through rebirth in human bodily form, the soul finds itself governed once more by the inexorable laws of terrestrial chronology.

APPENDIX II

Table of Historical Orbits

Born B.C.		Born A.D.		Orbital Period (years)	Mean Birth Date A.D.
1. Pericles	c. 490	Marlborough	1650	2139	630
2. Alcibiades	c. 450	Peter the Great	1672	2121	611
3. Aeschylus	525				
Aristophanes	448	Shakespeare	1564	2050	539
4. Plato	428	Hobbes	1588		
		Descartes	1596	2019	582
5. Aristotle	384	Leibniz	1646	2029	631
6. Socrates	470	Darwin	1809	2278	670
7. Phidias	490	Michelangelo	1475	1964	493
8. Philip of Macedon	382	Napoleon	1769	2150	694
9. T. Gracchus	163	Simon Bolivar	1783	1940	813
G. Gracchus	153				
10. Hamilcar Barca	270	Mohammed Ali	1769	2038	750
11. Hannibal	249	Ibrahim Pasha	1789	2037	770
12. Scipio Africanus	236	Wellington	1769	2004	767
13. Julius Caesar	102	Churchill	1874	1975	886
14. Mark Antony	83	Kemal Ataturk	1881	1963	899
15. Marius	155	Beaverbrook	1879	2033	863
16. Sulla	138	F. D. Roosevelt	1882	2003	880
Pompey	106				
17. Cicero	106	Duff Cooper	1890	1995	892
18. Catiline	108	Mussolini	1883	1990	888
19. Crassus	115	Stalin	1879	1993	882
20. Spartacus	c. 120	Lenin	1870	1989	875
21. Horace	65	A. E. Housman	1859	1923	897
22. Virgil	70	W. B. Yeats	1865	1934	898
23. Lepidus		Hitler	1889		

APPENDIX III

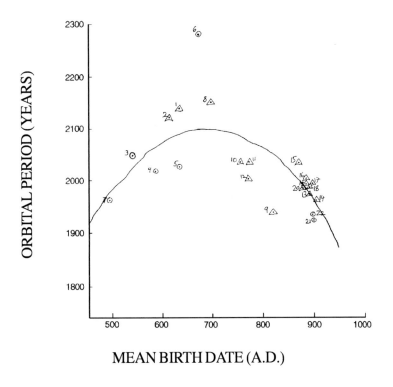

INDEX

Page numbers in italics refer to illustrations

Cooper, Lady Diana, 107,
176-181
Corinth,-ians, 40
Cornwall, 70
Crassus, 107-112, 137
Cresilas, 14
Cromer, Lord, 84
Cyprus, 158,160
Cyrene, 69

Damascus, 85
Danes, 77,78
Danube, 17,59,69
Darwin, Charles R. 65,*66*
David, King, 131-7
Demeter, 31
Demitius, 164
Demus, 49
Denmark, 36
Descartes, 54-62, *55*
Dionysius II of Syracuse,
54,57

East Anglia, 77
Egypt,-ian, 52,74,83,88-
91,98,139,141-2,144,148,
154,157,158-9,160,162,
164,166,168-9,171-3,177
Electra, 25
Ephesus, 151,152,161
Euclid, 56,61
Eumenides, The 46
Euphorbus i
Euripides, 25,49
Excalibur, 71,72

Falstaff, Sir John, 49
Florence, 68,123
Fourth Eclogue, The, 147
France, 54,56,74,85
Freemasonry, 122
Frogs, The, 49
Fulvia, 149,156
Furies, The, 45,46

Galilee, 123
Galileo, 59,64
Gaul, 107,118,129
Gaza, 85
Geminius, 162-3
Geneva, 30
Geometry, Descartes on, 61
Georgia, 110
Georgics, 119
German,-y, 73,74,111,136
Gordium, 70
Gracchi, the, 79-82
Graves, Robert, 173

Hamilcar Barca, 88,89
Hamlet, 47
Hannibal, 86-89
Haye, La, 54
Headlam, W, 42,45
Hebron, 133
Henry V, 49
Hercules, 148
Hermes, herms, 23,38,*39*,40
Hermetic Society of the
Golden Dawn, 122

Herod, 159,160,162
Hitler, Adolf, 138
Hobbes, T., 54-62,55
Holland, 59,60
Homer, 44
Homs, 85
Horace, 114-118
Housman, A.E., 115-118

Ibrahim Pasha, 83-91
Ides of March, The, 148
Indus, 69
Ireland, Irish, 120
Isaiah, 118,121
Isis, 147,152,163
Ismail, Khedive, 84
Israel,-ites, 71,127,133
Ital-y,-ian, 68,79,87,88,131,
   156,157,163

Jaffa, 85
James II, King, 14
Janus, 117
Jebusites, 133
Jeremiah, 118
Jericho, 159,160
Jerusalem, 85,133
Johnson, Dr. 142
Jonathan, 132,133
Josephus, 159
Judaea, Judah, 131,133,158-
   159
Julia, 135

Julius II, Pope, 123
Jupiter, 130

Kabbalah, 122
Kemal Ataturk, Mustafa, 99
Knights, The, 49
Konia, 85
Kremlin, The, 29,36

Lacedaemon *see* Sparta
Lancelot, Sir, 72
Langhorne, 151
Lefort, Franz, 30
Leibniz, 63
Lenin, 110-113
Lepidus, Aemilius, 128,130,
   137-139,150,157,160
Lesnaya, 33
Leviathan, The, 57
Livia, 135,171
Louis XIV, 17
Lucca, 109
Lucius, 156
Lucretia, 127
Lupercalia, festival of, 148
Lyceum, 63
Lycurgus, 25
Lysander, 27

Macbeth, 42-45
Macedon,-ian, 69,73
Maecenas, 118,119
Malmesbury, 54

Sicil-y,-ian, 23,41,52,54,62,
128,129
Sicyon, 74
Socrates, 18,21,30,34,49,52,
54,59,64-8,*66*
Solomon, 136
South America, 81
Spain, Spanish, 80,81,87,
89,108
Spart-a,-an, 9,22,24-27,37,
74,75,76
Spartacus, 112
Sphinx, the, 124
Stalin, 110
St. Jean d'Acre, 85
Stockholm, 62
St. Petersburg, 33
streltsi, 29,36
Streshnev, 28
Suetonius, 173
Sulla Felix, 99-102,
103,108
Sweden, 33,36,62
Syracuse, 40,54
Syria, 85,86,88,144

Tarquin the Proud, 127
Tarsus, 152
Tell-el-Kebir, 81
Terentia, 107
tetractys, 53
Theosophy, 122
Thrace, Thracian, 25,26,63,
162

Thucydides, 7
Tiberius, Emperor, 135-137
Timandra, 27,37
Tintagel, 70
Tissaphernes, 25
Troy, 23,43,44,
Turkey, Turks, 32,33,83-85,
90,99
Tuscany, 104

Ulm, 59,60
Uriah the Hittite, 136

Vatican, the, 123
Velleius Paterculus, 130
Venezuela, 80
Venus, 152,154
Vienna, 34
Vipsania, 135
Virgil, 114,118-124,147

Wahhabi tribes, 84,85
Waterloo, 88
Wellington, Duke of, 88
Wessex, 77
William the Conqueror, 97

Xantippe, 67

Yeats, W.B., 120-124

Zama, 88,90
Zeus, 69,70